Sexuality

CHOICES

GUIDES FOR TODAY'S WOMAN

Sexuality

Letha Dawson Scanzoni

The Westminster Press
Philadelphia

Book Design by Alice Derr

First edition

Published by The Westminster Press®
Philadelphia, Pennsylvania

PRINTED IN THE UNITED STATES OF AMERICA
9 8 7 6 5 4 3 2 1

Library of Congress Cataloging in Publication Data

Scanzoni, Letha.
   Sexuality.

   (Choices : guides for today's woman)
   Bibliography: p.
   1. Sex—Religious aspects—Christianity. 2. Women—Psychology. I. Title. II. Series: Choices.
BT708.S28 1984   241'.66   83-27375
ISBN 0-664-24548-X (pbk.)

To Becky,
    who was there when I needed her
    and whose empathy, encouragement,
    faith, love, and warm sense of humor
nourished and supported me through the most painful
and difficult period of my life. She has enriched my
understanding of friendship and sisterhood
immeasurably, and I am grateful.

CONTENTS

PUBLISHER'S ACKNOWLEDGMENT

The publisher gratefully acknowledges the advice of several distinguished scholars in planning this series. Virginia Mollenkott, Arlene Swidler, Phyllis Trible, and Ann Ulanov helped shape the goals of the series, identify vital topics, and locate knowledgeable authors. Views expressed in the books, of course, are those of the individual writers and not of the advisers.

CHAPTER 1

Experiencing Our Sexual Selves

Three-year-old Michelle came bursting out of the nursery school rest room to investigate some excitement in the classroom. In her rush, she neglected to pull up her panties and jeans—something her little friend Mark observed with interest.

"Girls don't have penises, do they, Dad?" he said to his father that evening. "No, they don't, Mark." His father held his breath slightly as he waited for Mark's next comment. "I know," the boy said, thinking back on the morning's discovery. "They just have stripes!"

Early in life, females and males realize their bodies differ from one another. A young girl looks in the mirror and sees folds and creases—the "stripes" Mark observed at nursery school. Sometimes, she and her brothers—already assuming boys' bodies to be the standard reference point—may think that something is missing in girls' bodies. This concern with "incompleteness" may show up in something as simple as the innocent remark of a two-and-a-half-year-old boy who told his parents he was going to get some sticks and a hammer and nails to build his new baby sister a penis. Or it may show up in a complex, sophisticated theory of "castration complex" and "penis envy," as set forth by Sigmund Freud and his followers. According to that theory, a boy fears losing his penis, and a girl wishes she had one.

One of the many helpful contributions of the contemporary women's movement, however, has been the insight that females are far less concerned about male penis deprivation than about male *privilege* deprivation. Females and males have been treated and esteemed differently in our society, with males considered to be of greater value. As Letty Cottin Pogrebin documents so well in her book *Growing Up Free: Raising Your Child in the 80's,* children become aware of this societal bias at a very young age and are convinced that boys are "better" and more important than girls.

And so, from earliest childhood, we are confronted with two basic ideas about human sexuality. They can be summed up in the words "difference" and "division." Children realize that boys have one kind of genitals, girls another. Because of that difference, humankind has been divided up into two categories: male and female. Rights, opportunities, privileges, responsibilities, and rewards have been assigned according to one's membership in one or the other of those categories. In fact, the very words "sex" and "sexuality" derive from a Latin term meaning "to divide or cut."

But these two basic ideas provide far too limited a view of what sexuality is all about. We simply can't stop with a mere acknowledgment of physical difference or the notion that such a difference inevitably spells division or even divisiveness—the much-joked-about "battle of the sexes." Surely the Creator never intended that our maleness and femaleness—reflecting God's image and pronounced "very good" (Gen. 1:27, 31)—should drive us apart rather than bring us together!

EXPANDING OUR UNDERSTANDING
OF SEXUALITY

Sexuality encompasses so much more than sexual anatomy or sex-role attitudes. It has to do with our entire *be*ing as body–spirit creatures. It involves our self-image, our body image, our self-esteem. It has to do with— perhaps more than anything else—our capacity for relationships, our desire for connectedness, our longing to be at one with somebody, our yearning to transcend our separateness. After all, the *only* pronouncement of "not good" in the Genesis creation stories occurred when God evaluated human aloneness. And it is through this capacity for union with another that *new life* springs forth (both biologically and figuratively speaking).

This yearning and capacity for connectedness does not, of course, mean that everyone will or should marry and that to choose otherwise is to be incomplete. In one sense, each of us is complete in ourselves, able to experience human wholeness *as an individual* created to bear the image of God in our own unique personhood. In another sense, we are lacking something without human companionship, because we were created social beings. But the point to be stressed is that we are not incomplete "halves" absolutely requiring marriage in order to be whole. Not to be paired is *not* to be impaired! Nor can marriage, for that matter, ever guarantee the banishment of aloneness. A marriage may end through separation, divorce, or death; and one finds oneself (in the words of a song popular in the seventies) "alone again naturally." Or a marriage may endure in name only and spell the loneliest existence in the world for one or both partners—even though the marriage exists for years or even decades.

So where does all this leave us in "experiencing our

sexual selves"? Probably with many questions, anxieties, and new thoughts struggling to come forward as we sort things out together. What we can say for sure is this: We were created sexual beings, and God pronounced our maleness and femaleness "very good." We were created in God's image as whole persons, regardless of marital status. And as sexual beings we were created for connectedness, created to be related.

But as we'll see throughout this book, genital relating is not the only kind of relating. Sexuality involves our ability as human beings to open our minds and hearts to one another and to give and receive in emotional intimacy as well as in physical intimacy. Sexuality also needs to be seen in connection with *sensuousness*—our capacity for enjoying and celebrating all kinds of bodily sensations, whether it be the fuzzy warmth of a new blanket, the bracing splash of a summer rain shower, the tender hug of a friend, or the playful nuzzling of a puppy.

GROWTH IN OUR SEXUAL AWARENESS

Experiencing our sexual selves is not a once-for-all occurrence, just as experiencing any other aspect of ourselves is not a once-for-all occurrence. All through life, we are in process—aspiring, struggling, growing, enjoying, hurting, enlarging our comprehension of human existence. If we're honest and open enough to recognize and admit it, we know we are constantly learning new things about our sexual selves—perhaps through a sudden awareness of our attraction to another person, or an undefined longing or sense of melancholy, or through reading a new survey or magazine article or participating in a study and discussion group, or simply by a personal reexamination of long-held assumptions about sexuality that we had never bothered to question or analyze before. At such times, it's important to put ourselves at ease and not berate ourselves with mental put-downs such as "I shouldn't be feeling this," or "I shouldn't think such thoughts," or "I must be a bad person to let such ideas cross my mind!"

An unfortunate part of our Christian heritage is a tendency to equate "bad" thoughts with sexual thoughts and "pure" thoughts with nonsexual thoughts. But again, we need to remind ourselves that *God* thought about sexuality in the first place, which means that thinking about sex can hardly be evil! Perhaps we would do well to think about sexuality the way the seventeenth-century astronomer Johannes Kepler thought about science. Kepler approached scientific study as "thinking God's thoughts" after God first thought them, tracing God's handiwork in an attempt to discover what the Creator had in mind in designing the world.

Similarly, we can try to learn what God had in mind for us in the creation of human sexuality. On the one hand, we can gratefully accept it as one of the good gifts God gave us to enjoy and enrich our lives. (See I Tim. 4:3–5.) On the other hand, because we live in a world that has been tarnished by sin, we see abuses of sexuality on every hand. In view of this, our thoughts will sometimes center around the negative ways sexuality has been perceived and used. We will want to be aware of such negative and destructive attitudes and actions so that we can do our part in helping to bring about change, or so that we can be prepared to deal with personal problems in these areas or to aid others who have in some way experienced sexual hurt.

But we'll probably find that our thoughts about sexuality are not confined to clear-cut positives and negatives. There always seem to be those *ambiguous* areas as well: the questions that don't have simple, unequivocal answers, the "certainties" that seem less certain than they once did.

Issues relating to sexuality seem to come up everywhere and at any stage of life. Perhaps we can see ourselves or someone we know in some of the following examples.

EXAMPLE NUMBER ONE:
NEW QUESTIONS IN LATER LIFE

The caller was nervous. "I'm a sixty-eight-year-old widow," she explained to the psychologist hosting the radio call-in program. "But I'm not living alone. For the past five years, I've been living with a very fine gentleman two years older than I. People assume we're married, and we really wish we could be. We *feel* married. But if I were to actually remarry, I'd lose my late husband's pension benefits and the hospital insurance protection I have. We can't take any financial risks in our circumstances. Yet I feel so guilty—so hypocritical. We want so much to go to church, but we don't feel we have the right to anymore."

The woman expressed her love for her Bible and her worries over the morality of her life-style. Never had she even remotely imagined having to deal with the questions of sexuality she was facing now at this stage of life. She spoke of the unfairness of the rules and regulations that were keeping her from legal remarriage.

The radio psychologist was understanding and compassionate. He told her that unjust laws do exist and that being "on the books" doesn't guarantee that a law is right or fair or even that it any longer serves the purpose for which it was originally intended. "Sometimes social laws and conventions don't take into account the complexities of human life and changing circumstances and thus they fail to serve human needs," he pointed out. The psychologist went on to assure the woman that the cohabitation arrangement adopted by her and her beloved partner was nothing more than an accommodation to the harsh reality that blocked their being legally married. "Go back to church," he told the woman, "and you needn't feel compelled to tell others of your situation. You are doing the best you can in very difficult circumstances."

EXAMPLE NUMBER TWO:
THE SHOCK OF RAPE

She was only a college freshman, adjusting to the newness of life away from home and not at all prepared for the shock of the long-distance phone call that night. It was her father, his voice trembling. He said her mother had been raped by a stranger who had brutally attacked her in her disabled car after offering to help. The doctors said she would be all right, but the whole family was terribly shaken.

The dazed student found her way back to her dormitory room and sobbed through the night. It would take several years and the help of a therapist before she could sense some emotional healing from the anguish she felt. She had recurrent nightmares, cried over the ordeal her mother had suffered, experienced deep rage at the realization that anyone could and would hurt her mother like that. She hated the man who did it, yet wondered where Christian teachings on forgiveness applied in cases like this. (Could God expect one to forgive a *rapist?*) The young woman felt that she must be strong for her mother's sake, providing her with support, nurturance, and courage in going on with life. But at the same time, the student longed to curl up on her mother's lap and be a little girl again, resting in her mother's strong arms and feeling her gentle caresses. She yearned for that sense of safety and security.

Then, one day, it struck her that the rape had forced

her to see her mother in a new way. She wrote about it in a poem:

> What is it that affects me most
> about this dreadful thing?
> Perhaps it's not the rape itself
> Perhaps it is my shame.
>   Today,
> I realized that my mother
>   is a woman
>   a feminine being
> that is different,
> much different
> from being a mother
>   somehow,
>   in seeing her as a woman
>   with a sexuality all her own
>   I realize that I too am a woman
>   with a sexuality all my own
> but we are the same
> we are one
> joined together
> by a bond that is now,
>   and for eternity,
>   unbreakable.
> (Name withheld. Copyright 1980 by the poet.
>   Used by permission.)

EXAMPLE NUMBER THREE:
SHATTERED DREAMS, DASHED EXPECTATIONS

In her late forties, the woman is disturbed by her husband's growing indifference toward her and his lack of interest in their sex life. They have been married for twenty-eight years, and their three children are now in college and in graduate school. The woman had looked forward to these "empty nest" years, expecting to enjoy a new sense of companionship with her husband. Instead, she finds the nest empty in a sense she never dreamed—

empty of her husband's devotion and desire for her. She finds herself wondering if he is having an affair but quickly dismisses the thought and feels guilty. "How could I even *think* such a thought?" she asks herself. "Everybody knows what a dedicated Christian husband and father he is. No, it must be something about *me*. Something must be wrong with me."

She eyes her body critically and—remembering some of his recent criticisms (though he called it joking)—decides to try losing weight. She looks for other possible ways to improve herself, even embarking on an information search to help her become a better sex partner to her husband. She reads as many self-help books and articles on sexuality as she can find. Then, after putting herself through her own cram course on lovemaking, reading about "pleasuring" and the "G-spot" and multiple orgasms and vibrators and countless ways to make herself attractive to her husband, she finds him no more interested in her than before. One day he comes home from work and says they need to talk. He announces that he wants a divorce. He is in love with a woman their older daughter's age.

EXAMPLE NUMBER FOUR:
DELIGHTING IN LOVE'S LONGEVITY

They are in their eighties and are as much in love as ever. "And we're just as interested in sex as when we were newlyweds," Arthur says with a laugh. "We just have a little problem."

Arthur and Ruby's "little problem" is Arthur's impotence, caused by diabetes, which has prevented their engaging in actual sexual intercourse for many years. "But we cuddle and snuggle and smooch and just enjoy holding each other." He chuckles. "And I can still set off the fireworks in Ruby," he says with pride. "I haven't lost my touch—and I haven't forgotten *where* to touch either!" His eyes twinkle as Ruby blushes. "I can make it seem like the Fourth of July around here!" he continues. Ruby pretends to slap his hand as she says, "You hush!" Then the two of them hug each other warmly, clasp hands, and laugh at their private little joke.

EXAMPLE NUMBER FIVE:
A STUDENT'S AGONIZING DILEMMA

Fourteen-year-old Jill asks her teacher if she can speak with her privately. She says she is having trouble concentrating on her schoolwork, that she has knots in her stomach, and that she is doing all she can to keep from sobbing right there in the classroom.

Jill confides that she is experiencing intense pressure from her boyfriend to engage in sexual intercourse. His closest male friend is dating Jill's best friend, and they too are pressuring Jill to give in to her boyfriend's wishes. That morning, Jill's best friend and several other girls had told Jill that they would no longer be friends with her if she didn't do as she was being requested to do and "give up her virginity."

Jill cries as she tells her teacher about the decision they expect her to make before the upcoming weekend. "I want my first sexual experience to be with someone I'm in love with. I want it to be special," she says. "And I really don't love him that way. Yet I don't want to lose him either, and I don't want my other friends to give up on me in disgust. I feel so torn! I just don't know what to do!"

EXAMPLE NUMBER SIX:
A NONCONVENTIONAL LOVE COMMITMENT

Gail leaned her head back and closed her eyes, pretending to be asleep. She didn't feel like engaging in conversation with the passenger seated next to her. The miserable weather and the delay in the flight schedule had added to the tension and exhaustion she felt from the weekend.

She winced in pain as she remembered her mother's harsh words. "I can't believe a daughter would hurt a mother the way you've hurt me, Gail. You're living in sin, and yet you want me to approve of what you're doing—give my blessing on a life-style the Bible condemns. You're sinning against God and against nature! I tried so hard to raise my daughters as Christians, and it wasn't easy with your father dying when you were still so young. So *this* is my reward!" She sighed and rested her face on the palms of her hands. "I need time to think, Gail," she said. "In the meantime, I'd rather you didn't come back home for a while. And I certainly don't want you bringing *her* here!"

Gail wiped away a tear as she thought back on her mother's anguished face and angry voice. Perhaps she had made a mistake in telling her what she had ached to tell her for so long. Even in her teenage years, Gail had known she was different from the other high school girls. She simply couldn't get interested in boys and dates the way they did. She had always, as long as she could remember, felt more of an attraction to the same sex than toward the other sex. Years later, at college, she met persons who spoke of themselves as "gay" or "lesbian," and she read a great deal on homosexuality, including new theological understandings of the topic. She talked to counselors, too, and gradually was able to acknowledge and accept her lesbian feelings.

Now, as a young professional woman, she had found a like-minded woman with whom she wanted to enter a lifetime committed relationship, much like the marriage of a man and woman—yet different in that they had no desire to follow or imitate the sex-role behavior of conventional marriage. Gail and Kay had found a minister who was willing to perform a religious ceremony of commitment for them. They wanted their parents to share their joy and had each gone to her parental home for the weekend to share her news. Gail had grown up in a strict, religiously conservative home and had known her mother might not accept her news with much understanding or empathy. Yet she and her mother had seemed so much closer in recent years and she had really longed to break down the barrier of secrecy, which had seemed so necessary for so long but which also had kept her mother from knowing her as she really was. Now Gail was having second thoughts. She wondered how Kay's weekend with her parents had gone. She could hardly wait to see her!

EXAMPLE NUMBER SEVEN:
LOVING REASSURANCE

The woman had undergone a radical mastectomy. The more she thought about it as she lay there in the hospital bed, the more she felt disfigured, ugly, deformed. She remembered past happy times of lovemaking. She remembered her husband's teasing whistles and soothing caresses and his comments about how perfectly formed her breasts were. Now her left breast was gone. She wondered if he would still find her sexually attractive. But she couldn't bring herself to ask him.

As he held her hand in the hospital room that night, he sensed her anxiety. He brought up the subject, and they talked honestly about their feelings. Kissing her tenderly, the woman's husband assured her of his deep, unchanging love for her and spoke of the beauty he saw in her no less now than in the past. Her attractiveness to him had not in the least been diminished by the removal of a diseased body part.

"I'm just so thankful to have you with me, darling," he said. "Had they not discovered this malignancy, had they not performed the surgery, I might have lost you! That's all I think about or care about. I have you with me! We're

together, sharing a life together. That's what matters."
He looked into her eyes intently. "That's *all* that matters." He reached over to the vase of roses he had
brought, pulled out a bud, and lightly pressed it against
her cheek. "You're as beautiful in my eyes as this rose,"
he said. "And you always will be."

MORE TO COME

These stories may elicit various reactions from us.
Their purpose is to focus our attention on the many ways
women experience aspects of their sexual selves in daily
life. Some experiences are positive, some negative, some
perhaps puzzling. But one thing is sure. Such experiences are common to all of us. We need not feel alone,
alienated from ourselves, others, and God, because of our
sexuality. Remember, sexuality—with all its questions
and feelings—is a universal experience. Remember, too,
that God designed our sexuality. Let's go on to explore
what a theological, scientific, and practical understanding of that design might mean for us.

CHAPTER 2

Our Sexual Understanding

A Ziggy cartoon shows Ziggy standing alone, gazing out a window and bemoaning the fact that he has spent his entire life "preparing for a world that doesn't seem to exist."

No doubt we've all felt like Ziggy at times. Some readers grew up at a time when it at least *seemed* that most people felt the same way about sex. There appeared to be a consensus about what was wrong, what was right, what wasn't to be talked about, and what seemed too sacred, too special, too mysterious, too personal, or even too "dirty" to be studied. One did not try to find out what other people were doing, or thinking, or wishing, or fantasizing, or worrying about sexually. That's why the Kinsey studies of the forties and early fifties came as such shockers to so many people. It wasn't only what they revealed about the sexual behavior of American women and men; it was that such studies were conducted at all!

Those who grew up in those more restrictive times now see a world quite different from the one they prepared for. Some may wish they could go back to those times when the questions were few, the answers simple, and society held out a clear-cut script for the "good women" with whom men settled down—women the men chose to be their devoted, dutiful wives and the praise-worthy mothers of their children.

Others shudder at the thought of ever returning to those times. They are persuaded that societal norms and the hush-hush attitude cheated them of their sexual birthright by favoring male fulfillment in every area of life, sex included. They may now be wondering if they missed something and were denied opportunities to live up to their full sexual potential.

Some women have mixed feelings as they watch their daughters and granddaughters asking questions they never dared to ask and living in ways they never dared to live—because "nice girls" didn't ask certain questions and were expected to steer clear of behavior that raised other people's eyebrows, even though such behavior might seem quite acceptable and harmless now.

I remember the shocked attitude of one elderly woman who told me of the "indecent" behavior of her thirty-five-year-old son and his wife. "They actually take showers together!" she exclaimed, assuring me that she and her husband would never have dreamed of such a thing as bathing together. In fact, they had never seen each other's nude bodies, though they were now in their seventies.

Similar extreme modesty showed up in one of the letters newspaper advice columnist Ann Landers received in 1983. A troubled husband wrote that his strict, religious wife even threw a towel over the digital alarm clock so that the glowing numbers wouldn't cast light on their united bodies during sexual intercourse. Other husbands have complained that their wives always dress and undress in a bathroom or closet.

Television talk show host Phil Donahue once remarked that many of us were taught: "Sex is dirty. Save it for the person you marry." When it's put that way, it's easy to see the absurdity and contradiction in such teachings. Yet countless women swallowed such admonitions without allowing themselves to think about their full impact. That impact, many found, came later. Not being permitted to seek information about and come to an understanding and acceptance of their sexuality caused some women to feel guilt over their sexual fantasies or masturbation, or showed up in an inability to reach orgasm in marriage, or resulted in fears that their experimentation with varied sexual techniques might be an indication that they or their husbands were in some way abnormal.

On the other hand, other readers grew up in more recent times and have known a more sexually permissive climate. But they too may be finding that the world they thought they were preparing for didn't turn out to be what they expected. The sexual permissiveness is there to be sure, they will tell you, but it isn't delivering all that it promised. There's the herpes scare, for example. Many young adults are now seeing that casual, recreational sex with a variety of partners can be risky and costly.

Then there's the psychological pressure from peers. High school- and college-age women are finding that in some circles it's considered as much a disgrace to be sexually *in*experienced as it was to be sexually experienced years ago. The "world of sexual freedom" evidently isn't any more real than Ziggy's expected world. After all, if we don't have freedom to say "no" when we really want to, we don't have *freedom*. Instead, we are still feeling controlled from the outside, living according to other people's wishes and rules for us.

"The problem," says one woman, "is that you're made to feel strange and abnormal if you aren't ready to go to bed with someone even before you've had a chance to get acquainted." Middle-aged and widowed, she longs for the less sexually pressured days of her own courtship experience years ago.

"The whole atmosphere is so sexually *charged*," someone else points out. "I mean, look at the songs, the advertisements, the soap operas on TV, the movies, the sexual innuendos at work and at social gatherings. I'm not a prude, but yet I don't like sex screaming at me *constantly!* Give me a break! I almost wish for the old Victorian silence about sex."

But that wasn't so great either, an eighty-year-old woman reminds us. "I wish I had known even a small part of what younger people know about sex today. There's so much I still don't know. When my daughter got married, it was *I* who was asking *her* questions rather than the other way around. I figured she would have read some books and could help me with some problems her dad and I were having. When I was growing up, there were many things we women wondered about and worried about, but we couldn't feel free to talk about such intimate matters—even with other women. Today it's so different."

But is it? Many women say they still don't feel free to voice their sexual questions, joys, anxieties, and experiences (whether positive or negative). That's one reason many seem eager to respond to magazine surveys on sexual attitudes and experiences or attend workshops on women's sexuality. Psychotherapists Lonnie Barbach and Linda Levine, who conduct educational and therapy workshops for women, were struck by the way women attending them were eager to use one another as sounding boards, relieved to find other women just like themselves who could be resources for questions, insights, and reassurance. Even as late as 1980 when their book *Shared Intimacies: Women's Sexual Experiences* was published, it struck these authors "how unusual it was for this exchange of information to be taking place in our culture."

Shere Hite, in preparing *The Hite Report* (1976), found the same thing. Typical of respondents who answered her questionnaire was the woman who wrote, "I am grateful because finally I got to tell how I *really* feel about sex and my sex life." The woman said it was like having a burden lifted to be given a chance to talk about sex frankly and honestly. For others, answering the survey questions provided an opportunity to learn more about themselves. Others hoped the long-range impact of the study would shed light on how women actually experience their sexuality (as contrasted with what men have *told* women that women should feel about sexuality), thus sparing women the agonies of feeling inadequate, different, frigid, somehow lacking—and alone and isolated from the experience of other women.

WHY WOMEN HAVE FOUND IT DIFFICULT TO TALK ABOUT SEX

Women whose religious background emphasized a negative view of sexuality may have an especially difficult time talking about the topic. (More on that in the next chapter.) But at least two other factors are involved in the inhibitions many women feel. The first has to do with our biological makeup.

Learned Unfamiliarity with Our External Genitalia. Little boys become familiar with their penises from their earliest years. They giggle and want parents to watch proudly as they aim a stream of urine as though they were holding a fire hose. Their major reproductive equipment (penis and testicles) is easily located. But for little girls, it's different.

A little girl's ovaries, fallopian tubes, uterus, and

vagina are tucked away inside her body where she isn't aware of them. As for the *external* genital area, even many grown women aren't quite sure how to refer to it. They may still, as adults, speak of it in vague terms such as "down there" or their "private parts" or "female parts." One middle-aged woman remembers asking as a child what to call this part of her body, which she observed to be so different from her brother's. Her mother told her it was her "do-funny"!

The correct name is *vulva*. A woman's vulva consists of folds of skin called the outer lips and the inner lips (the *labia majora* and the *labia minora*, if you care about Latin terms). The outer lips are thicker and hair-covered. The inner lips are much thinner and are especially sensitive to sexual stimulation.

The vulval area contains two openings, the *opening for urine* to pass through and the opening to the *vagina*, the passageway which receives the penis during sexual intercourse and through which the baby is expelled during the birth process. It is through the vagina that the monthly menstrual flow passes, too.

The major female sex organ of pleasure, the *clitoris*, is located in the front part of the vulval area. Society's reluctance to acknowledge women's sexual pleasure is a second reason that discussing sex has been hard for many women.

Societal Attitudes Toward Female Sexuality. The taboos against examining and handling the external genital area are strong for girls. In the case of boys, for whom the organ of sexual excitement and pleasure is also the organ for excreting urine, taboos against handling and viewing the penis would be senseless and impossible. (Of course, some parents do have anxieties about "too much" handling beyond necessary bathroom functions. In one extreme case reported by Helen Colton in her book *Adults*

Need Sex Education, Too, a mother sought to ward off a
small boy's temptation to masturbate by telling him that
his penis—which she called his "teapot"—would fall off
if he played with it too much. To drive home her point,
she told the boy that was why the little neighbor girls
didn't have "teapots"!)

Women have traditionally been taught a sense of
shame and embarrassment about touching the vulval
area or viewing it in a mirror (which could help them
understand better how God has designed this part of
their bodies). Some women have reached their adult
years not knowing what the clitoris is or what it exists for
and have mistakenly believed it contained the opening
through which the urine passes.

One woman, having learned well her mother's and
aunts' embarrassment about touching one's body "down
there," was so upset and revolted by her physician's
recommendation that she use a diaphragm that she
accidentally slammed her car into another car at a stop-
light as she drove home to tell her husband about it. "I
couldn't bear the thought of having to insert the diaphragm," she says.

Until recently, it wasn't considered desirable for wom-
en to have sexual feelings, let alone *admit* to having
them. Women had to do a great deal of pretending and
denying in order to keep both their hymens and their
reputations intact before marriage and assure their husbands of their virtue afterward.

But even if it is acknowledged today that females have
sexual needs and feelings no less than do males, traditional sex-role socialization is still around in large measure. Boys have been taught to think of sex in a more
detached way—as an end in itself rather than in the
context of a loving relationship with great emotional
involvement. Girls grow up learning to think about sex
less as an end in itself (even though the pleasure is

certainly admitted) and more as an important ingredient in a committed and loving relationship. Society still wants females to be the gatekeepers, expected to control how far males may be permitted to go. Increasingly, voices of protest are heard about the unfairness of it all, and young males especially are being urged to see their own responsibility in sexual matters (including contraception). But far too often, males have been given the impression early that what matters in sex is pleasure, performance, a sense of conquest ("How far can I get with her?"), and peer status ("Did you score?"). For females, questions uppermost in many minds are "I wonder how much he cares about me," "Does he love me?" or "I wonder if he finds me attractive."

Differences in how women and men tend to view sex may show up not only in dating but later in marriage as well. Again, it's important to keep in mind that this results more from sex-role training (how we're taught to feel and act as females and males) than from our physiological differences.

THE SEXUAL REVOLUTION

Although some people quibble over the terminology and argue that an *evolution* (gradual change) rather than a *revolution* (abrupt overthrow of established ways) has occurred, few would deny that sexual values and behavior have changed greatly in this century.

What are some of these changes? For one, premarital sexual intercourse is far more common than was once the case and begins at an earlier age. Over the decade of the seventies, social scientists Melvin Zelnik and John F. Kantner conducted a number of large-scale, scientifically reliable, and representative studies of the sexual and contraceptive behavior of adolescent women in the United States. In a report prepared for *Family Planning*

Perspectives (Sept./Oct. 1980, pp. 230–237), these researchers presented the finding that half of today's unmarried fifteen- to nineteen-year-old women have experienced sexual intercourse. In 1971, this was true of fewer than one out of three young women.

Among the 50 percent of teenage women engaging in sexual intercourse, the average age of the first experience was sixteen. Zelnik and Kantner's most recent study also included *unmarried young men* aged seventeen to twenty-one (since the sexual partners of the young women were found to be about two years older). Their 1980 report showed the premarital sexual intercourse experience for the males to be 70 percent.

This study also revealed that, by the time they are nineteen years old, 69 percent of unmarried women have engaged in sexual intercourse, as compared to 46 percent in 1971. (Kinsey and his associates reported in 1953 that they found that 20 percent of the women in their sample had experienced sexual intercourse by twenty years of age.)

When Kinsey and his colleagues conducted their studies, they found indications that an abrupt shift in the sexual behavior of women took place around the time of World War I. Those who reached young womanhood around that time and into the "Roaring Twenties" had a nonvirginity rate of 50 percent, though a considerable proportion of them had sex only with the men who became their husbands. These were women born after 1900. Women born *before* 1900 were found to have had much less premarital sexual experience, with only one out of four no longer a virgin at the time of marriage.

After that abrupt change, premarital sexual intercourse rates remained much the same until recent times. During the half century of time between the 1920s and the 1970s, the changes had more to do with *attitudes* (more openness about sex, less condemnation of premarital sex—especially in serious love relationships, even if the wedding date wasn't close at hand) and increases in *other types of sexual behavior,* most notably petting. (Intimate touching and fondling of sexually excitable parts of one another's bodies provided a way to experience the ecstasy of orgasm without "losing one's virginity." This was the period of time when discussions of "technical virginity" were prevalent.)

Many other changes were taking place, too—changing attitudes toward birth control, homosexuality, cohabitation, masturbation, abortion, sex research, and a new appreciation of sex in marriage. But the biggest changes have been in the recognition that women are sexual beings who have a right to their own sexual choices and destiny. We have seen indications of this already in the increase in premarital sexual experience among young women. (Because of the prevalence of the double standard, the percent of the premarital experience of males has remained around the same—roughly 70 to 85 percent—throughout this century. Thus the male statistics have come as no surprise to most people.)

Certain aspects of the sexual revolution have raised ambivalent feelings among some women. Linda Wolfe, who wrote *The Cosmo Report* (1981), reports that the finding which struck her most from the *Cosmopolitan* magazine survey on sex attitudes and behavior was that slightly over half the 106,000 readers who responded to the survey felt that the sexual revolution had gone too far. They felt sex had become too casual and too expected on dates. They felt pressured and coerced by men who never called them again if they refused various sexual activities. They suspected that what had been promised as sexual "liberation" for women may have been a plot by men to obtain sexual pleasures more easily. Wolfe said that the "sexual discontent" expressed in the survey was especially striking since Cosmo women are not known for being prudish, inexperienced, or sexually inhibited. They tend to be women who enjoy their sexuality but resent the new tyranny, which says they *must* have sex—not out of free choice but because it's demanded of them.

On the other hand, another popular magazine survey showed positive gains for women, prompting the editor in chief of *Ladies' Home Journal,* Myrna Blyth, to conclude that "the sexual revolution's greatest effect may be on sex *within* marriage." She was commenting on the conclusions of psychology professor Ellen Frank and articles editor Sondra Forsyth Enos, who analyzed the 83,000 questionnaires received from readers who responded to the magazine's survey on "The Lovelife of the American Wife." They wrote in the February 1983 issue (p. 119):

> The vast majority of our respondents see a healthy, active sex life as a natural and important part of being married. We can only speculate that because they know more than their mothers and grandmothers did about the physiological aspects of sex—and because they have heard over and over again that pleasurable lovemaking is a wholesome and appropriate goal—they are enjoying sex more than any previous generation of women ever did. (© 1983 by Family Media, Inc. Reprinted with permission of Ladies' Home Journal)

Their comment about "knowing more" leads us to a final point on this chapter's theme of *understanding our sexuality.*

FEMALE SEXUALITY: WHAT WE NOW KNOW

Scientific advances and a more open climate for conducting sex research have brought to light findings that provide women with much reassurance and validation of their own experience of their bodies.

The design of the female body indicates that God intended that women should not only provide pleasure for their husbands and conceive and give birth to children but that women themselves should experience the exciting and explosive joy of sexual ecstasy.

At least, that would be our conclusion about the Creator's intent if we look at just one simple fact about female sexual physiology: *only women have a sexual structure that has absolutely no other function than to provide sexual delight.* As Masters and Johnson point out in their pioneering research report, *Human Sexual Response* (Chapter 5), the clitoris—that small protrusion enfolded in the lips of the vulva—exists for the sole purpose of receiving and transforming sensual stimuli. It has nothing to do with excretion or reproduction (both of which are true of the male penis). The clitoris is there simply to cause women to feel good during sexual expression and release.

Nothing should seem more obvious than the observation that women experience sexual pleasure and the recognition of the role of the clitoris in that pleasure. Yet tremendous controversy has been generated around these topics. In the Victorian era, sexual pleasure in women was thought to be nonexistent or at least undesirable. Good women weren't supposed to have sexual feelings; they were simply to provide good feelings for their husbands. (Some nineteenth-century women took issue with this idea, as we will see in the next chapter.)

Women's experience of sexual pleasure through the clitoris has especially come under the fire of criticism. Freud taught that young women first become aware, through masturbation, that the clitoris is an organ of pleasure. But if the woman is to move on to true femininity, according to Freudian thought, she must subordinate the feelings of the clitoris and switch the area of sexual responsiveness to the vagina. Clitoral orgasmic response was considered "immature" as well as "unfeminine." A woman considered to be frigid was one who could not achieve orgasm through the penetration of her vagina by a man's penis.

And so untold numbers of women, worried about being abnormal, unfeminine, immature, and frigid, rushed to the offices of Freudian psychoanalysts to find out what was wrong with them and why they couldn't respond properly to their husbands. Most of all, they wanted help in achieving the mystical, magical, but ever-elusive experience of the "vaginal orgasm."

Already, in their 1953 volume, *Sexual Behavior in the Human Female*, Alfred Kinsey and his colleagues argued that an attempt to make the vagina "the center of sensory stimulation" is doomed to failure because such a transference is a physical impossibility. These scholars criticized those psychoanalysts, marriage counselors, and others who, by "ignoring the anatomic data," inflicted much psychological suffering on women. The Kinsey researchers attempted to drive home their point by calling attention to the fact that most women's vaginas are lacking in "end organs of touch" (necessary nerves) and thus are insensitive—a fact of which gynecologists were well aware, as shown in their performance of surface surgery on the vagina without using anesthesia.

Why then were so many people willing to deny the evidence (and, in the case of women, deny their own experience) in order to believe a myth? The answer appears to be a combination of defining sexuality from a male point of view and an acceptance of a "natural law" type of understanding of sexual intercourse. It was probably thought that the way that the male and female bodies fit together in nature's design for the ongoing of human life decreed that each would receive pleasure in a way that corresponded with the fitting together. To use a farfetched analogy, it would be like saying that since a train "enjoyed" being in a tunnel, the tunnel "derived its pleasure" from having the train there!

However, two major research findings in recent years have provided compelling reasons to lay the old clitoral-transference-to-vaginal orgasm notions to rest. First, the laboratory research of Masters and Johnson showed the primary role that the clitoris plays in female orgasm, regardless of whether the orgasm occurs through direct clitoral stimulation, during the general overall love play surrounding sexual intercourse, or in the act of intercourse itself. Their research showed that there are not two separate entities which can be neatly labeled "clitoral" versus "vaginal."

Second, the exploding knowledge in the fields of embryology and genetic research helps us to realize that, in sexual feelings and response, males and females have far more in common than was ever imagined previously. Of special importance is the finding that the penis and the clitoris grow from exactly the same "root" in the human fetus. As medical researchers John Money and Anke Ehrhardt point out in *Man and Woman, Boy and Girl*, the outward appearance of the male and female genital area is exactly the same until the eighth week of fetal life. The tiny genital tubercle that will become a clitoris or penis and the tiny "urogenital slit" are no different in what will become either a boy baby or a girl baby; they "have the capacity to differentiate in either direction."

If the penis and clitoris have the same beginning, it is not surprising that they are analogous in makeup and that each is richly supplied with nerve endings designed to bring sexual pleasure.

No wonder, then, that Masters and Johnson found the basic stages of sexual arousal through sexual climax to be so similar in both female and male orgasm. No longer can it be said that females lack the capacity for sexual enjoyment. In fact, it could be argued that in one sense they have an even greater capacity, based on the Masters and Johnson finding that women's physiology permits them to have more orgasms within a shorter space of time than is possible for men.

An awareness of the primary importance of the clitoris does not mean that the vagina makes no contribution whatsoever to the act of sexual intercourse. Some women speak of the great psychological pleasure it brings them to feel so close and connected to the man they love. Some women have enhanced their own and their husbands' pleasure through special exercises that strengthen the vaginal muscles—a series of vaginal push-ups, so to speak. The popular Kegel exercises develop the muscle that women use when they stop a flow of urine; they're described in Lonnie Barbach's helpful book, *For Yourself: The Fulfillment of Female Sexuality.* In recent years, there has also been a revival of interest in the Grafenberg spot, popularly known as the "G-spot." This is a small mass of what appears to be erectile tissue around the tube that carries urine from the bladder. In some women, it can be felt through the wall of the vagina and is sexually sensitive. Lonnie Barbach's *For Each Other: Sharing Sexual Intimacy* contains a brief and simple discussion of this area.

CHAPTER 3

Our Sexual
Theological Heritage

"I really resent what my strict religious upbringing did to me," Pam said, a mixture of anger and hurt showing in her eyes. "Here I am, thirty-four years old, and I still can't feel at home with my sexuality. All those old messages keep going around in my head like a recording: 'Don't touch. Don't talk about that. Don't think those thoughts. Don't read that. Don't see that. Don't *feel!*' There are so many good books I was forbidden to read that would have helped me feel more positively about sex, I'm convinced. But the church I was attending until recently tries to control by intimidation everything its members do, read, listen to, think about, or question. And anything having to do with sex is especially taboo."

Pam's feelings are echoed by many persons who grew up with the idea that sexuality and religion are at odds with each other. On the other hand, among the *Ladies' Home Journal* readers who responded to the survey mentioned in the preceding chapter, religion showed up as a positive factor in marital sexual satisfaction. Many wives credited their faith with the overall sense of well-being that enabled them to appreciate and enjoy their sexuality.

What can we conclude? Only this. For some women,

religious beliefs are liberating and help them celebrate their sexuality. For other women, religious beliefs are oppressive, causing them anxiety, shame, and distress. It all depends, of course, on what one's religious beliefs are.

A woman who believes that sex is a good gift of God, created for pleasure as well as procreation, will have a view of sex quite different from a woman who believes that sexual intercourse was the forbidden fruit in the Garden of Eden which plunged the whole human race into sin because Adam and Eve tasted it!

THE BIBLE SPEAKS POSITIVELY
OF WOMEN'S SEXUALITY

Long before Masters and Johnson, Lonnie Barbach, *The Hite Report,* and all the other books and articles affirming the sexuality of women, the Scriptures spoke of the playful, delightful joy experienced in the loving embrace of two persons committed to share a life together. Women were considered to be every bit as sexual as men. Commenting on how firmly that belief has been held throughout Jewish history, Rabbi Maurice Lamm expresses amazement that Western thought took so long to recognize women's sexuality. "The Bible conceives of sex within marriage as the woman's right and the man's duty," asserts Lamm in his book *The Jewish Way in Love and Marriage* (1980, p. 136). Such a notion is, of course, the direct opposite of Victorian notions about sex.

In Judaism, for a man to marry a woman and then ignore her sexual needs is a violation of religious duty. Lamm refers to the serious study the later rabbis devoted to the *mitzvah* ("good deed" or "commandment") that requires husbands to care for their wives' sexual needs. These scholars sought to understand the full meaning behind the *mitzvah,* which was based on the three duties of husbands mentioned in Ex. 21:10–11 (providing food, clothing, and a wife's conjugal right to sexual intercourse) and the passage in Deut. 24:5, which speaks of a man's being excused from the ancient military draft during the first year of marriage so that he could stay home and "rejoice his wife."

The rabbis concluded that the sexual expression ordained as the wife's right must not be merely a mechanical act—an emotionally detached husbandly duty. Rather, they emphasized, the sexual expression must be accompanied by closeness and by joy. Furthermore, "both of these qualities require *gavra,* the involvement of the total personality, not merely a physical performance" (*The Jewish Way in Love and Marriage,* p. 31).

Of course, wives were expected to care for their husbands' sexual needs, too. The man who was tempted to scatter his sexual energies among strangers was told to keep them for the intimate and delightful embrace of the marriage bed.

> Let your fountain, the wife of your youth,
> be blessed, rejoice in her,
> a lovely doe, a graceful hind, let her be your
> companion;
> you will at all times be bathed in her love,
> and her love will continually wrap you round.
>   (Prov. 5:18–19, NEB)

Perhaps the most outstanding (and, to many persons, *astounding*) celebration of female sexuality in the Bible is the entire book of the Song of Solomon. It is a poetic description of the sheer ecstasy experienced by a couple as they mutually delight in the sexual embrace. This is not the story of a man who initiates and "acts" and a woman who passively receives and is "acted upon." Quite the contrary! Not only are *both* constantly giving and receiving in the act of love, but the entire poem is written primarily from the woman's point of view.

Both know what it means to be *lover* (one who loves) as well as *beloved* (one who is loved, the very term speaking of the universal hunger to *be loved*). In my sex education book for the Christian home, *Sex Is a Parent Affair*, I have suggested ways the description in this love poem sets forth the biblical ideal for sex within marriage, which is nothing short of "joyous sexuality."

The Song of Solomon is rich in energy and imagery. The woman speaks; the man speaks; and a chorus of women, "the daughters of Jerusalem," are there to listen, observe, and comment—much as a Greek chorus offered comments on the stage action taking place in the ancient Greek dramas, which are still frequently performed today. "Eat, O friends, and drink: drink deeply, O lovers!" the chorus tells the couple (S. of Sol. 5:1b).

This book of the Bible speaks forthrightly and positively about sensual delights. The depth of longing for the one loved, the phenomenon of "love-sickness" (2:5), the thrill of erotic touch and sight, the excitement of hearing the loved one's voice, the wonder of exploring each other's bodies, the joy of smelling the fragrant perfumes and sweet spices, the taste of tender and passionate kisses, the lush beauty of the garden of love, the anguish and pain over separations, the playful spontaneity, the total absence of shame and inhibition, the sense of belonging ("My beloved is mine and I am his" [2:16]; "I am my beloved's and my beloved is mine" [6:3].), the appreciation of being friend, companion, sister, and brother as well as spouse to each other, and the firm conviction that many waters cannot quench such a love as this—all this and more greets us in this "song of songs."

Yet "it is a song the church sings with an uncertain voice, if it is sung at all," say the study committee members who drafted a denominational report for the

United Church of Christ (*Human Sexuality: A Preliminary Study,* 1977, p. 64). They refer to the traditional interpretations that limit the Song of Solomon's meaning to *symbolism*—an allegory of the spiritual life—while evading the literal *erotic realism* that has so much to say to the reader.

ATTITUDES TOWARD SEX OVER THE COURSE OF CHURCH HISTORY

Much of the problem stems from negative attitudes toward the body, sexuality, and women throughout much of church history.

In the Old Testament, the human body is praised as a marvelous creation of God. The psalmist said to God, "It was you who created my inmost self, and put me together in my mother's womb; for all these mysteries I thank you: for the wonder of myself, for the wonder of your works" (Ps. 139:13–14, JB).

And in the New Testament, the human body receives its highest honor in the doctrine of the incarnation: the eternal Christ comes to us in human flesh (John 1:14; Heb. 2:14 and 10:5–7). Further, we are told to think of our bodies as temples of the Holy Spirit and to glorify God through them (I Cor. 6:19–20; Rom. 12:1–2).

Yet many early church leaders who were most vocal on issues of sexuality were men influenced by a Greek dualism that separated body and spirit and saw them in opposition to each other. The body and anything material was viewed as inferior and a hindrance to the higher life of the soul. In some philosophies, matter was considered not simply inferior but *evil.* Anything having to do with the body (such as sex) was considered spiritually defiling.

Such philosophical teachings, with their emphasis on self-denial and mastery over the body's needs and desires, were often carried to extremes and gave rise to an ascetic spirit among the Christians influenced by them. Even marriage was viewed with suspicion and negative feelings because of the sexual component. This occurred in spite of New Testament warnings about those who would forbid marriage and certain foods, forgetting that God's creation was intended for enjoyment. "For everything that God created is good, and nothing is to be rejected when it is taken with thanksgiving, since it is hallowed by God's own word and by prayer" (I Tim. 4:4–5, NEB).

During the first several centuries of the Christian church, some ascetic Christians went to great lengths to show their disdain for their bodies and urged others to follow their example and strict teachings. Again, they were forgetting biblical teachings such as this passage from Col. 2:21–23 (NEB): "Why let people dictate to you: 'Do not handle this, do not taste that, do not touch the other'—all of them things that must perish as soon as they are used? That is to follow merely human injunctions and teaching. True, it has an air of wisdom, with its forced piety, its self-mortification, and its severity to the body; but it is of no use at all in combating sensuality." Believers were to remember that they had a life in Christ which was to determine their behavior—not the keeping of arbitrary rules.

The early church leaders not only showed evidence of the influence of certain Greek philosophies, they were also reacting against the "anything goes" attitude toward sexuality prevalent in their cultures. They felt that abuses of sexuality had to be curbed, and they wanted to establish Christian ethical standards which contrasted with those of the people around them who didn't know and serve God. In this, they were following the lead of the apostle Paul, who had written about this same matter in his first letter to the Thessalonian Christians (I Thess. 4:1–8).

However, to confound matters further, several of the early church fathers had themselves led sexually indulgent lives before their conversion to Christianity. They regretted their loss of virginity and the "sinful lusts" of their youthful adventures, the memories of which were hard to erase. In spite of prayer, tears, and fasting, sexual feelings and fantasies would arise unbidden even after the knowledge that their lives had been surrendered to Christ. These Christian leaders apparently didn't know what to do with such feelings, had difficulty integrating them with the Christian life, and yet felt a great urgency to make pronouncements to others on how *they* should conduct their sexual lives. This was not true in every case, of course, but it happened enough to cause some modern theological writers to speculate that at least some of the views that have influenced Christian attitudes toward sexuality may have emerged from various leaders' struggles to come to terms with their own sexuality.

At any rate, much of the material from Christian leaders of the early centuries and into the Middle Ages indicates great anxiety and even revulsion over sexual matters. Wishes were expressed that God had planned a less embarrassing method of reproduction than sexual intercourse with its "bestial movements" and explosive passion. The sex organs were spoken of as "ugly" and as disfigurements, thoughtfully provided by God because of God's foreknowledge of the Fall, when humans would become "like animals." Some persons found it particularly abhorrent to think about the location of the genitals and their intermingling with the body's excretory functions.

Great distress was voiced especially over the involuntary nature of sexual arousal and its accompanying physical signs—most notably the male erection. It was like having a part of the body with its own will! Jerome wrote of the agonies he went through in trying to subdue his "rebellious flesh." Augustine wrote at great length about sexuality as he imagined it would have been in the Garden of Eden before the Fall, "because not yet did lust move those members without the will's consent," and Adam and Eve could thus be naked and unashamed. But when sin entered the world and they "were stripped of grace, that their disobedience might be punished by fit retribution, there began to be in the movement of their bodily members a shameless novelty which made nakedness indecent" (*City of God*, xiv).

Church leaders grudgingly acknowledged sex in marriage to be necessary so that children could be brought into the world, but they urged restrained and infrequent sexual intercourse. Couples were to abstain from sex for several days before partaking of the Eucharist. By the Middle Ages, teachings about sexuality, even in marriage, had gone to lengths that can't help seeming absurd today. Some theologians warned married couples that the Holy Spirit left the bedroom while the couple engaged in sexual intercourse. Some suggested that one of God's *greatest miracles* was in making such a defiling act sinless when used for procreation within the sacrament of marriage.

Penitents were told they must not engage in sexual intercourse during holy seasons and special feast days as well as before partaking of Holy Communion. But in addition to these restrictions on married couples, Yves of Chartres instructed the devout to abstain from sexual intercourse on Thursdays and Fridays in remembrance of Christ's capture and crucifixion, on Saturdays to honor the Virgin Mary, on Sundays to commemorate Christ's resurrection, and on Mondays out of respect for departed souls.

Commenting on these teachings, Rabbi Maurice

Lamm contrasts the attitude shown here with the Jewish outlook on sexuality among medieval scholars. Friday night, the beginning of the Sabbath, was recommended as an ideal time for a husband and wife to come together in the sexual embrace. Holiness and sexuality are thus linked. "The joy of sex is not vulgar and merely tolerated," writes Lamm. "It is a joy appropriate to the holiest day of the week, a physical joy that is not merely the delight of the spirit" (*The Jewish Way in Love and Marriage*).

Attitudes toward sexuality were also linked to attitudes toward women over the course of church history. Males had mixed feelings about females—at times condemning, fearing, and reproaching them as sexual temptresses who seduced men away from spiritual matters, and at other times insisting that women were asexual guardians of virtue who didn't care about or enjoy sex or even have sexual feelings and desires.

Foreshadowing what has come to be known as the "madonna-prostitute complex" (the tendency of some men to separate women into desexualized "good women," on the one hand, and "bad women" who enjoy sex, on the other), some religious leaders spoke of women's twofold "use" as harlotry or maternity. Women were told to hide their beauty—or even appear ugly—to protect men from the arousal they felt in the presence of beautiful women. The stirring up of sexual passions was not thought to be the man's problem but rather the woman's, for "causing" his feelings.

With the Protestant Reformation came a greater acceptance of the naturalness of sex as a God-given and mysterious power granted to human beings and intended to be experienced in marriage. But the Reformers worried about problems of lust and a lack of control in a fallen world and urged sexual restraint both within and out of marriage. Martin Luther, whose views on sexuality and marriage underwent changes over the course of his writings, at one point compared marriage to a hospital where persons with strong sexual urges could be admitted for the healing of sinful lusts.

The idea that sexual desire was an "infirmity" was common in the thinking of these theologians. Marriage was seen as the "remedy" provided by God. After all, hadn't the apostle Paul written, "It is better to marry than to be aflame with passion" (I Cor. 7:9)? It was true that God had created human sexuality to be something honorable and holy; the Reformers affirmed this wholeheartedly. But, as John Calvin pointed out, this same sexuality could burn out of control as a result of sin's entrance into the world. There was now the danger of "burning immoderately," which Calvin saw as "a fault arising from the corruption of nature." However, he went on to say in his commentary on the Corinthian epistles that "in the case of believers, marriage is the veil by which the fault is covered over so that it no longer appears in the sight of God."

At the same time, religious leaders recognized other ways to think about sex in marriage. In 1650, an English member of the clergy named Jeremy Taylor spoke of the reasons married couples engaged in sexual intercourse. In his book *The Rule and Exercises of Holy Living*, he listed "a desire for children, or to avoid fornication, or to lighten and ease the cares and sadnesses of household affairs, or to endear each other."

The New England Puritans, known for their sober and austere outlook in many areas of life, nevertheless were quite realistic about the sexual expression of love between husband and wife and did not hesitate to put high value on "endearing each other." Their only concern was that earthly love should never be allowed to be put above love for God. And they would have agreed with the writer to the Hebrews who spoke of marriage and the marriage bed as honorable but spoke of God's judgment on nonmarital sex (Heb. 13:4). They held high standards for sexual expression, but they were never squeamish or prudish about sexuality in and of itself.

The Victorian period (the time of Queen Victoria's reign in Great Britain, 1837–1901) was a time of prudery, extreme observances of conventionalities, and a great deal of sexual hypocrisy. It is the Victorians, not the Puritans, that we have to thank for the sense of shame and embarrassment over female sexuality that has come down to us. Pornography and prostitution were widespread during the Victorian period in England and were winked at as legitimate outlets for male sexual needs. Good wives, on the other hand, were expected to be virtually sexless except for fulfilling their maternal roles.

Victorian thought was no less prevalent in the United States. "The best mothers, wives, and managers of households know little or nothing of the sexual pleasure," wrote a turn-of-the-century author and lecturer. "Love of home, children, and domestic duties are the only passions they feel. As a rule, the modest woman submits to her husband, but only to please him" (T. W. Shannon, *Eugenics*, 1904).

Some women had already been taking issue with such ideas in the nineteenth century. The notion that good women were not *supposed* to have sexual feelings but were simply to provide good feelings for their husbands struck them as absurd. Mary Gove Nichols, a campaigner for health reform, asked if it would not have been "a great injustice" for God to "so constitute woman as to suffer the pangs of childbirth with no enjoyment of the union that gives her a babe." In a book entitled *Marriage*, she argued, already in 1854, that "healthy nerves give pleasure in the ultimates of love without respect to sex." If women didn't find pleasure in sex and were indifferent toward it or found it repugnant, it meant that the nerves designed to bring pleasure were exhausted or diseased because of unhealthy conditions and too frequent childbirths.

Near the end of the nineteenth century, Elizabeth Blackwell (who, against great odds, had become the first female physician in the United States) reasoned similarly. She too referred to women who were considered to be "proof" of the natural lack of feeling and interest in sex that characterized women. Blackwell explained: "These women have been taught to regard sexual passion as lust and as sin—a sin which it would be a shame for a pure woman to feel, and which she would die rather than confess. She has not been taught that sexual passion is love, even more than lust. ... The growth and indications of her own nature she is taught to condemn, instead of to respect them as foreshadowing that mighty impulse towards maternity which will place her nearest to the Creator if reverently accepted." (Blackwell, *The Human Element in Sex,* 1894 ed.)

THE SEXUAL EQUALITY OF WOMEN AND MEN

Women who are ashamed to think of themselves as sexual beings, women who deny or repress their sexual feelings, wives who fear being too bold or aggressive and would never dream of taking the initiative in sex relations with their husbands, women who feel they must wait to be "acted upon" if they are to be truly feminine and who hesitate to be fully involved participants in the sexual expression of love, girls who are told during their dating days that they bear the responsibility for setting limits because they don't have the strong and urgent sexual drives that boys have—these and other members of the female sex, regardless of age, need to hear the truth. Sexual shame and the denial of female sexuality do not originate in the Bible at all. Such notions stem from the distorted views of early church leaders—who saw the human body as less than spiritual and found its impulses frightening and abhorrent, especially in the sexual realm—and from the Victorians of the last century.

When we turn to the Bible itself, we see a recognition of sexual desire in both women and men and an emphasis on mutuality and equality in the sexual relationship. The apostle Paul made this clear in his instructions to the Corinthian Christians:

> A man should fulfill his duty as a husband, and a woman should fulfill her duty as a wife, and each should satisfy the other's needs. A wife is not the master of her own body, but her husband is; in the same way a husband is not the master of his own body, but his wife is. Do not deny yourselves to each other, unless you first agree to do so for a while in order to spend your time in prayer; but then resume normal marital relations.

> (I Cor. 7:3–5, TEV)

We have already seen the recognition of equal sexual desire and enjoyment in the relationship described in the Song of Solomon. Perhaps one last point should be mentioned from that biblical love poem. In her book *God and the Rhetoric of Sexuality,* Old Testament scholar Phyllis Trible points out the change that occurs in love *redeemed* as contrasted with the tragedy of male domination that occurred as the result of the Fall. The first woman was told at that time that her desire would be for her husband but he would "lord it over" her (see Gen. 3:16, JB). Trible writes (p. 160):

> In Eden, the yearning of the woman for harmony with her man continued after disobedience. Yet the man did not reciprocate; instead, he ruled over her to destroy unity and pervert sexuality. Her desire became his dominion. But in the Song, male power

vanishes. His desire becomes her delight. Another consequence of disobedience is thus redeemed through the recovery of mutuality in the garden of eroticism. Appropriately, the woman sings the lyrics of this grace: "I am my lover's and for me is his desire" [S. of Sol. 7:10].

By turning directly to the Scriptures, we may find some surprises. We discover that our true theological heritage in sexual matters has been clouded over by erroneous ideas without any basis in biblical ideals. This realization, along with a growing awareness of new research findings on biological and psychological aspects of female sexuality, can be tremendously liberating and can lay the groundwork for a personal value system in making sexual decisions throughout our lives.

CHAPTER 4

Our Sexual Values
and Decision-making

"It all used to be so simple," Kate said. "The rules were clear-cut. You—and everybody else—knew what was right and what was wrong. Sex was supposed to be reserved for marriage, *period*. It was wrong before; it was right afterward. The whole thing came down to a matter of timing."

"Yes, that was it exactly," Marie chimed in. "Do you remember that illustration some ministers used when they wanted to make that point in the fifties? They'd compare sex to the rich, brown soil that was so beautiful and functional in the garden. But if someone brought a shovelful of that same soil into the house and dumped it on the floor, it stopped being beautiful and became just plain *dirt*. Our preacher said that's what sex outside marriage was—dirt. But that it was beautiful in its right place. I know he was trying to be helpful, but he never told us how to make the transition. How do you go about transforming dirt into beauty?"

"You don't."

The voice was Christine's, and the others looked up with surprise. Christine took another sip of coffee before she continued.

"The whole premise behind that illustration is faulty.

Not only does it fall into the old 'sex is dirty' trap that so many of us are still trying to get out of at some deep psychological level. It also depersonalizes sex. It makes it a *thing*, an object. Sex isn't something you shovel! It's something you *feel*. The illustration is too mechanistic, too dehumanized. Young people today would think it's ridiculous. They're talking about meaning in sex, not timing."

Kate interrupted, "I think you're being too idealistic again, Christine. Judging from the remarks and jokes I hear from my students, things aren't that much different than they were in our high school years. Kids laugh about sex, brag about it, seem preoccupied with it. They're fascinated by the topic but find it a bit scary, too, in the beginning. The peer pressure's much greater. But kids are out for a good time, and I don't think they're thinking much about some ethereal, abstract 'meaning.' The boys are out to get all they can, and the girls are concerned about having 'sex appeal.' Some things never change. This generation of teenagers believes it discovered sex— the same as our generation did. The feelings that are new and exciting to them are assumed to be new in the history of the world!"

Jan, who had been quiet until now, spoke up. "I hear what you're saying, Kate. And I think you're right—up to a point. But I agree with Christine too. The whole social climate has been changing, and I think people *do* think about sex differently now. I sense a difference in the discussions at the university. That's one of the side benefits of going back to finish your college education at forty-four! You get to hear firsthand how the younger generation is thinking." She paused and laughed and then continued.

"One of the biggest changes is the increase of options and decisions that have to be faced these days. My daughter was telling me about a conversation she and some of her friends were having in the dorm the other night. They said that a young woman used to have to decide only whether or not she'd go all the way before marriage—with all kinds of social supports to encourage her to wait. Now she feels pressure to be sexually active *early* and in a way totally separate from anything having to do with marriage—I mean, it's not a matter of being engaged and close to a wedding date with this one-and-only who'll be your husband anyway.

"So that's *decision number 1:* Should she be sexually active? Then, if she decides yes, there's *decision number 2:* What kind of contraception should she use—or will he use something? Then there are the decisions about whether or not to live with her boyfriend and if and when she should ever marry. And what about children? Should she have any at all—and, if so, how many? Should she postpone having them until she's well established in her career? And then, what about her 'biological clock'? Will she be too old to have children if she waits? My daughter said, 'Mom, you had it easy. Marriage, sex, and children were all one package when you got married. For us, it's a whole battery of agonizing life decisions.' But she does make one point that fits in with what Christine was saying. She says that her friends talk about *quality* and *depth* in relationships. Some of them think they can find that through sexual experiences. Others aren't so sure."

FREE CHOICE AND SEXUAL STANDARDS

The questions raised in the conversation among the four friends we've just been listening in on are questions many of us are concerned about. Perhaps we're concerned about them as we make our own sexual decisions. Perhaps we're concerned about them as teachers, pastors, counselors, and parents who want to transmit religious values and provide wise guidance for the children and young adults we care about. But whatever the reason for our concern, they are questions we know we can't dodge in today's world. And if we want to be informed Christians and integrate our faith with life *as it is* (and not simply as we might wish it to be), we'll want to give some attention to sorting out these issues.

It may help to clarify matters if we turn to a book published in 1960 entitled *Premarital Sexual Standards in America*. Its author, sociologist Ira Reiss, wanted to go beyond looking at premarital sexual *behavior*—which had been studied by many other social scientists—and concentrate primarily on sexual *standards*. In other words, what attitudes, beliefs, and values lie behind decisions to engage in sexual activities before marriage—or not to?

Reiss had noticed that in the 1950s many college textbooks for courses on marriage and the family implied that sex before marriage was by its very nature separated from love and tenderness and based instead on lust, promiscuity, and self-centered gratification of sexual appetites. While any observer would be quick to agree that such depersonalized, body-centered sex takes place in countless instances, such a sweeping generalization did not seem to fit the whole picture as Reiss saw it. He felt there was much more to the premarital sexual scene, and he devoted twelve years of research to exploring ways people feel about it.

Reiss found that most people tend to hold one of four sexual standards that coexist in the United States today. Our society's formal standard is *premarital sexual abstinence*. According to this standard, sex before marriage is wrong for both women and men under any and all circumstances. However, a second standard has been around as long as the abstinence standard; that's the *double standard*, which says premarital sex is all right for men but not for women.

The two remaining sexual standards were of special interest to Reiss because they were not being recognized in writings on premarital sex even though their acceptance by considerable numbers of unmarried and formerly married persons was obvious to anyone who took a close look at the topic. Both standards were permissive, in that sex before marriage was *not* considered unquestionably and absolutely wrong. And both standards were egalitarian, in that both women and men were considered to have the same rights to sexual enjoyment apart from marriage, in contrast to the old double standard.

Reiss called the first of these two newer informal sexual standards "permissiveness with affection" and the other one "permissiveness without affection." Persons who held a *permissiveness with affection* standard believed that premarital sexual intercourse was right for both men and women if they felt strong affection or love for the partner, especially in a stable relationship such as engagement.

In contrast, persons who held to *permissiveness without affection* did not feel love was necessary to justify premarital sexual intercourse. What mattered was physical attraction and a desire to engage in sexual intercourse for the enjoyment it brought. It could be recreational sex—just something a person enjoyed doing with another person, like playing tennis. Or it could be a way of saying "I like you and really had a good time with you this evening," but without any expectation of building a stable, ongoing relationship. This way of looking at sex was also considered right for both women and men— although its most popularized version, what came to be known as the "Playboy philosophy," appealed more to men. Women had been taught to associate sex with affection, and the idea of separating the two wasn't something they could accomplish easily. At the same time, there were some women who were eager to embrace the standard and experiment in the name of a newfound acknowledgment of female sexuality or as a statement in the "back to nature" and "sexual freedom" movements of the sixties and early seventies.

After Reiss had classified the four basic sexual standards among which young adults were apparently choosing, other social observers pointed out certain variations and new rules of the game—such as taking care not to exploit sexual partners, making sure that both parties were operating under the same sexual standard so that no one would be hurt, developing an etiquette for discussing and dealing with such matters as contraception and the avoidance of sexually transmitted diseases, and so on. But what was clear to the vast majority of persons by now was that the old ways of thinking about the subject were no longer adequate. No longer was it simply a matter of sex outside marriage versus sex inside marriage. One had to ask what *kind* of sex outside marriage was taking place. Which premarital sexual standard was being followed? What was the meaning of sex to the participants?

Furthermore, with all their questioning of social institutions during the sixties, young people weren't willing to accept at face value the assertion that sex outside marriage was always impersonal and body-centered, while sex inside marriage was automatically deeply caring and person-centered. They knew of instances where unmarried sex was loving and meaningful to two persons devoted to one another; and they also knew of instances where married sex was unloving, perfunctory, exploitative, manipulative, and sometimes even cruel. The matter of actual marital rape had to be admitted, too, even though it wasn't yet discussed much in the news media. In other words, keeping the soil in the garden didn't guarantee that it couldn't still be dirt!

It wasn't that young people were totally rebelling against marriage. It was just that they could see things weren't so simple and clear-cut as their elders had told them. And they wanted honesty, not pretense and hypocrisy.

They also wanted some say in their own destiny, a sense of control over their own lives. "Past sexual standards were developed by parents—by those in authority," wrote Reiss. "These standards were devised, consciously and unconsciously, so as to make the 'best' match for offspring." But the situation had been changing since the late 1800s, with a growing emphasis on individual choice and personal happiness and with the selection of a mate being made on the basis of *love* rather than according to the wishes of two sets of parents concerned with merging families and controlling the distribution of money and property. Even so, young people continued to try to keep and adjust to the sexual standards they had inherited. "Now a new code is being fashioned and, for the first time, by young people themselves," Reiss commented in his concluding chapter on future trends. "Since they are the ones to choose their mates, they must also decide how to act in courtship. Because the new code is being devised by young people, it is concerned with their problems and desires." He suggested that the sharpest contrast from the past is seen "in that sexual behavior is now almost fully separated from pregnancy and marriage, if one so desires" (*Premarital Sexual Standards in America*, pp. 246–247).

Something else has been happening in the current social climate. Whereas at one time premarital sexual activity signified the *loss* of something (namely, virginity), it is now likely to be perceived as a *gain*—a gain in peer status, a kind of "rite of passage" into adulthood, an expansion of self-knowledge. To a certain extent, this has long been true in the male peer culture ("Haven't you tried it *yet?* Man, you haven't lived!"). But this attitude has now become increasingly common in the friendship cliques of young women and in the general youth culture from junior high (and even younger) through college and in the singles scene—and extending into the "single again" culture as well. The two key ideas seem to be a continuing openness to new experiences and a constant quest to find and fulfill one's true identity. Sex is seen as a means to these ends.

SOME BIBLICAL GUIDELINES

It may well be that too much is being expected of sex today. To expect to discover one's true self through the experience of an orgasm is to put too much freight on an important aspect of life that was never intended to carry so heavy a load! The self is so much more than experiencing the union of genitals, which explains why so many people are disappointed in their sexual encounters today. They expected so much more than the experience delivered, no matter how enjoyable it seemed at the time. And so they go looking for that one more unique experience that will surely be what they're looking for— much as the ancient writer of Ecclesiastes, who tried everything possible in his search for meaning but concluded that it was all "like chasing the wind." What was left unfed, of course, was the soul's hunger for God, which can never be satisfied by wealth, sex, work, success, fun, or openness to every possible adventure and experience. There is a very real sense in which we can only experience our true self and know who we really are by knowing the One who made us and discovering God's intention for us. Rather than searching for an elusive "self," we can join Paul in saying, "I press on, hoping to take hold of that for which Christ once took hold of me" (Phil. 3:12, NEB). Then other things have a way of falling into perspective, sex included, so that we don't elevate them to an importance they were never intended to have. It would be so easy in our day and age to make sex into an idol that consumes our attention and energies and has us persuaded we can't live without it. We need to remind ourselves of Paul's words, "Your life is hid with Christ in God" (Col. 3:3), so that we don't chase after the wind seeking our life—our true self— elsewhere.

Perhaps that is why the biblical writers emphasized sex in the context of *covenant*—a covenant modeled after the covenant between God and the people of God. To know oneself and to know another human being cannot be accomplished in one brief moment, one pleasurable act, one transitory experience. True knowledge, true relating (which is, after all, part of the search today), takes time.

The people of Israel understood the concept of cove-nant to involve several ingredients: a *promise* (the pledge of loving care and faithfulness), *continuity* (a shared destiny, which meant a future to look forward to together and a history to later look back on and cele-brate), and a sense of *belonging* to one another in the richness of a relationship that promised security and growth in the ongoing experience of knowing the loved one. God's love provided the ideal, as shown in this passage of Scripture:

> I will betroth you to myself for ever,
> betroth you with integrity and justice,
> with tenderness and love;
> I will betroth you to myself with faithfulness,
> and you will come to know Yahweh.
>
> (Hos. 2:19–20, JB)

These qualities of *continuity and faithfulness* (provid-ing a sense of safety, security, and stability); *integrity, justice, fairness, and equity* (providing assurance of no exploitation, no "using" someone for one's own benefit);

and *deep, caring, compassionate love, empathy, and tenderness* lay the groundwork for the union of bodies that the term "one flesh" signifies in Scripture. To try to approximate that "one flesh" meaning through sex alone, apart from the context of the covenant relationship, is to dilute its meaning. (See I Cor. 6:12–20.)

Christians who are looking for a way to think through their own personal values and sexual standards do not need to think in terms of restrictions and rules. All they need do is ask themselves what they want from their sexual experiences. Do they want *casual sex* for the sake of the experience alone, without regard for relating on anything more than a physical level? Or do they want *companionship sex,* in which there is some sense of warm friendship feelings or romantic desires toward the other person but no pledge of faithfulness, no intent of continuity, no desire to share all one's life as well as one's body? Or are both these standards somehow lacking? If so, the biblical ideal of *covenantal sex* may be the answer.

CHAPTER 5

Our Sexual Anxieties and Longings for Intimacy

We live in a sexually anxious age. The news media; our families, friends, and other personal acquaintances; the themes of modern novels, plays, movies, television programs, and songs; possibly even our own lives—all make us aware of this anxiety.

Our anxieties tend to center around our body image, sexual capabilities ("performance anxiety"), sexual interest, sexual orientation, and a fear of aloneness. We long for intimacy, and all too often we have accepted without question that intimacy and sex are synonymous—or that the way to intimacy is through the meeting of *bodies* rather than the meeting of persons in their totality and at the deepest level of their beings.

OUR BODY IMAGE

How we feel about our bodies quite naturally has a great deal to do with how we feel about our sexuality. The norm in our culture dictates that a slim body is a sexy body. (It has been different at other times: witness the paintings of large-bodied sensuous nude women during the Renaissance period.)

Although some encouraging signs have shown up in

recent years (movement away from the widespread use of pencil-thin models in advertisement; interest in aerobic dance, in weight lifting, and in other athletic workouts as a way to good muscle tone, health, and body shaping, for example), the thinness standard has resulted in an alarming increase in serious eating disorders. Some young women—and a smaller number of young men— are so fearful of weight gain that they jeopardize their health, starving themselves to the point of emaciation.

Their eating disorder is called *anorexia nervosa.* Malnourished, having lost a significant percentage of their body weight, and with a gaunt, skeletal look, they nevertheless see a distorted image of obesity when they look at themselves in a mirror. Such an eating disorder contributed to the cardiac arrest that took the life of singer Karen Carpenter in early 1983.

Other young women purge their bodies through vomiting or the use of diuretics or laxatives after interspersing their self-starvation patterns with "eating binges." The fasting, binging, and purging eating disorder is known as *bulimia.*

Both anorexic and bulimic women are excessively worried about getting fat and have an exaggerated need to feel in control of their own bodies. Such women tend to be overly critical of themselves and are often painfully sensitive to the real and imagined evaluations of other people. They ignore their bodies' own messages and try to force themselves into a rigid body mold that is not only unsuitable for them but downright dangerous.

The problem stems in part from an unwillingness to recognize and appreciate the enormous variety in God's creation. Gloria Steinem, founding editor of *Ms.* magazine, once wrote about her experience at a health spa ("In Praise of Women's Bodies," *Ms.*, April 1982). During the few days of the spa program, women of all ages gradually overcame their modesty and accepted casual nudity among themselves in the kinds of situations males have long experienced—steam room, locker room, showers, and so on.

As the women became comfortable in one another's presence, they developed a new appreciation for the uniqueness of each individual woman's body. Gone were bras, panties, other undergarments, and swimsuits, which can be "visual reminders of a commercial, idealized image that diverse female bodies rarely fit," Steinem wrote. She spoke of the acceptance the women felt of themselves and of each other as they observed stretch marks from pregnancies and incision scars from cesarean sections, hysterectomies, and other surgery.

At the end of her spa experience, Steinem reached this conclusion:

> I doubt that fat or thin, mature or not, our bodies could continue to give us such unease if we learned their place in the rainbow spectrum of women and humanity. Even great beauties seem less distant—and even mastectomies and other realities seem less terrifying—when we stop imagining and begin to see.
>
> (*Ms. Magazine*, April 1982, p. 32.
> Used by permission.)

Of course, women aren't alone in worrying about their body image. While women worry about the size of their breasts (Are they too small? Are they too large?), men may be worrying about the size of their penises (even though size of the nonerect penis indicates nothing about sexual capabilities). Both females and males need reassurance of the wide variation among human beings. Women who worry about the normality of their clitorises also need reassurance of the range of diversity in size, coloring, shape, degree of covering by the hood, and so on. The drawings and photographs in the Federation of Feminist Women's Health Centers' book *A New View of a Woman's Body* can be very helpful in this regard.

A poor body image can have a negative impact on sexual interaction. In an article published in *Medical Aspects of Human Sexuality,* a professional journal for physicians (June 1980), medical school professor Sheila Jackman points out that persons who are anxious about their bodies tend to be emotionally distracted during times of sexual intimacy. They worry constantly about what the sexual partner must be thinking about them and their perceived physical imperfections. Jackman says that, as a result of the mind's focusing attention away from erotic pleasure during such times, natural physiological responses are hampered or remain uncultivated and the person fails to experience sexual enjoyment.

We need to accept ourselves as God's creation and learn to feel good about ourselves as persons dearly loved by God—and that includes accepting our bodies. If we can love ourselves, loving others will come much more easily. Both the Old and New Testaments emphasize loving our neighbor *as we love ourselves* (Lev. 19:18; Matt. 22:37–40; Gal. 5:14; Jas. 2:8). If we keep berating ourselves for not being taller, shorter, thinner, more curvaceous, "sexier," or simply prettier (however we may define the terms), the mental put-downs will rob us of the energy we need for loving others and building good relationships. Regardless of physical attributes, warm, caring, joyful, enthusiastic, life-affirming people are going to be considered attractive in the eyes of those who care about what matters in life.

SEXUAL CAPABILITIES

In a market-oriented society, it often seems that everyone is being held up for sexual scrutiny. We have already looked at the concern about appearance and the underlying question, "Am I acceptable?" Closely related to it is another question: "Am I able? Can I perform adequately sexually?" Because some sexual partners think of sexual intercourse in terms of performing and achieving rather than as depth-relating, sex can take on the qualities of work rather than of pleasure and can bring much anxiety.

In one extreme example, a woman wrote to advice columnist Ann Landers to complain of her hurt at discovering that her husband was keeping scorecards on how well she was doing in both her cooking and her sexual performance. He had devised a five-star rating system (ranging from "excellent" to "rotten") and joked about showing his wife's ratings to his friends at work! The wife was becoming so nervous about what grade she would be given each time that she could no longer enjoy their sex life (column of April 5, 1983).

In an article on "sexual scorekeeping," psychiatry professors Josef Weissberg and Alexander Levay suggest that rating systems provide a ritualized way of using sexual experience for the purpose of nonsexual ends (*Medical Aspects of Human Sexuality*, Nov. 1979, p. 13). Among the nonsexual objectives they name are the attempt to prove oneself attractive and desirable, the hope of shaking off a haunting sense of personal inadequacy and low self-esteem, or viewing sexual performance as an opportunity for expressing competitive drives and power strivings. Scorekeepers do not want to be vulnerable to another person and thus shy away from intimacy. Instead, they are obsessed with numbers: numbers of orgasms, numbers of sexual acts, numbers of sexual partners, and so on.

Some sexual anxieties women experience are associated with the performance and score-keeping ways of thinking—either on the part of their partner or themselves. Such persons are hoping that sexual experiences will validate their worth in some way or give them a

sense of personal power that is lacking in other areas of
their lives.

Jenny, for example, is a woman with such a low self-
image that she feels she has nothing to offer but sexual
favors. She looks upon the sexual adventures she has had
with various men (including several married men) as
proof that she is at least desirable in this way—even if no
one is interested in any kind of overall relationship with
her or commitment to her. In her occupational life, she is
doing quite well; but in her personal life, sex has become
a crutch. It gets her through her anxieties about finding
some sort of fulfillment in a social life. After all, she
reasons, look how many men have wanted her!

Brenda, on the other hand, feels anxious because of her
husband's concerns about sexual success. If, because of
fatigue or stress or some other reason, he is not able to
"perform" sexually, he is devastated, and Brenda's day or
evening is ruined as well by his irritable or sulking
mood. On the other hand, he expects her to "perform" as
well. He considers her having an orgasm as his achieve-
ment. He works hard toward this end, not for the sake of
satisfying Brenda but as a measure of his own skills as a
lover—as a man. Brenda finds it increasingly hard to
relax during their sexual activities. She tenses up and
often is unable to reach orgasm—which causes her husband finally to give up in anger and disgust. Brenda
would often be content with tender, loving moments of
cuddling and snuggling at such times. But her husband
can't see it that way; he sees sex entirely in terms of
success or failure, the same way he sees his business
ventures.

Sometimes we doubt our appeal as sexual partners
because we look to some other person as a "mirror"
without realizing that the particular mirror reflects a
distorted image because of that person's own insecurities
or power strivings. Irene's feelings of worthwhileness as

a sexual partner were deflated when her husband repeatedly made fun of her large breasts (which had made her self-conscious and an object of teasing remarks ever since junior high days, and her husband enjoyed his jokes even though he knew this was a painfully sensitive issue with her). Lynnette was crushed when her husband of thirty years told her that her vagina was "too loose and flabby" to bring him sexual pleasure any longer. Perhaps without realizing it, such men are saying more about themselves than about their wives. They are certainly not acting as reliable mirrors for judging one's self-worth.

Some sexual anxieties about capabilities relate to the area of "sexual dysfunctions—sexual problems with either psychological or physical causes, which can usually be helped through sex therapy, marriage counseling, or medical treatment, depending on the nature of the problem.

The most common sexual problems for men are *erection difficulties* (inability to have an erection or to sustain it) and two kinds of *ejaculatory difficulties:* (1) rapid ejaculation soon after entering the woman's vagina, or even before penetration, with the result that the partner feels it's over before she has even begun, and (2) an inability to ejaculate at all during sexual intercourse.

For women, the most common sexual problem is an inability to experience orgasm. Often the problem can be solved quite simply through exercises in masturbation—the treatment most often recommended by sex therapists. Lonnie Barbach's book *For Yourself* tells how a woman may go about learning to be aware of her body's sexual capacities and to enjoy sexual pleasure without shame and embarrassment in the privacy of her own home. A companion book for couples, Barbach's *For Each Other,* tells how the two persons can communicate to each other what means most to them sexually so they can work together for solutions in certain problem areas. Many husbands and wives, even after years of marriage, are still afraid to tell each other their likes and dislikes in the marriage bed. They need to overcome long-standing fears and inhibitions, often stemming from childhood teachings that "sex is dirty" and is not something to be talked about.

Certain other sexual problems of women can also be solved quite easily—for example, insufficient lubrication of the vagina. Using a water-based lubricant jelly, available in the feminine hygiene section of any drugstore, usually takes care of the problem. Ordinarily the natural lubrication of the vagina indicates sexual arousal in a woman, just as an erection is the major sign of sexual arousal in a man. But women vary in the amount of lubrication they have, and many find that it decreases as part of the aging process. In addition, birth-control pills or various medications can affect lubrication. Psychological factors contributing to nonarousal may also need to be explored in some cases.

Insufficient lubrication is one of several factors that may be involved in uncomfortable or even painful sexual intercourse. Both men and women may experience painful intercourse (called *dyspareunia,* in women) for many different reasons, and a careful medical examination is crucial in seeking out any possible physical reasons for the difficulty.

Vaginismus is another problem some women have. The vaginal muscles tighten and go into spasms, causing the vagina to clamp shut so that penetration by a penis is impossible. Often this is related to anxiety of some kind—performance anxiety, for example, or feelings of guilt about having sexual intercourse even in marriage. In a number of cases of vaginismus studied by Masters and Johnson, a strict religious outlook was characteristic of the women, as it was of several of the men they treated for an inability to ejaculate in their wives' vaginas (*Hu-*

man Sexual Inadequacy, Chapters 4 and 9). Marriages have remained unconsummated for many years because of such problems.

Couples need not cheat themselves by ignoring or denying these problems when help is available. They are not alone in their difficulties, and they need not feel embarrassed or ashamed. Trained counselors can help them find solutions, because more is now known about sexuality than ever before.

Even persons faced with the challenge of a serious physical disability can find creative ways to enjoy an active, pleasurable sex life. Societal prejudices have often labeled physically disabled persons as asexual, which is cruel and insensitive. Rehabilitative medicine departments of hospitals and medical schools can provide helpful information on a broad range of sexual experiences possible for persons with genital impairments due to cancer surgery, persons with spinal cord injuries, persons with cerebral palsy, persons with multiple sclerosis, and any other illness or surgical procedure that causes concern about sexual functioning. The Sex Information and Education Council of the U.S. (SIECUS, 80 Fifth Avenue, Suite 801-2, New York, NY 10011) publishes an inexpensive annotated bibliography of helpful resources on sexuality and disability.

Persons facing some form of ostomy surgery should know about the reassuring, informative, low-cost booklets on sexuality available from the United Ostomy Association, 2001 Beverly Boulevard, Los Angeles, CA 90057. *Ostomy* simply means "surgical opening" and refers to surgeries where an abdominal opening has been made for the elimination of bodily wastes because of a disease, injury, or birth defect that makes normal bowel or bladder functioning impossible.

SEXUAL INTEREST

Some sexual anxieties spring not so much from sexual problems and challenges as from attempts to measure ourselves according to some arbitrary standard of "normality" or some notion about what everybody else must be doing sexually. (In quite another context, the apostle Paul wrote of those who "are without understanding" because "they measure themselves by one another, and compare themselves with one another" [II Cor. 10:12]. His observation applies here!)

We are all different. Our degree of sexual interest differs and may be influenced by various factors that raise or lower it under different circumstances and at different times of life. Similarly, couples vary in the frequency in which they engage in sexual intercourse. There is no "correct" number of times per week. What pleases the individual couple is what matters. If one partner desires sexual relations more often than the other, loving communication and compromises can work the problem out. The same is true of trying out various sexual positions and techniques. Some couples, for example, find oral-genital sexual contact a meaningful expression of love. Among other couples, one or the other or both may react negatively to the very idea.

Such matters as sexual techniques and practices in the privacy of a couple's own bedroom are matters of personal preference, not morality—unless, of course, somebody is being hurt. It's wrong for one partner to coerce the other into doing something the other finds repugnant or physically or psychologically painful, or to make the other feel degraded and humiliated in some way. Otherwise, a couple's way of expressing themselves sexually is between the two persons and God and is nobody else's business. Don't forget the imaginative, joyful lovemaking of the Song of Solomon!

SEXUAL ORIENTATION

Still another kind of anxiety relates to the question of sexual orientation—the *direction* of our sexual feelings. In other words, do we find that our erotic love feelings are basically directed toward someone of the same sex or of the opposite sex? Are we homosexually or heterosexually oriented? Gail and Kay, the lesbian couple in our opening chapter, illustrate this type of anxiety.

It hurts to be labeled "sick" or "sinful" for experiencing love feelings that spring from one's core being and bring enrichment to one's own life and the lives of others, deepen love for God and humankind, and release pent-up creative energies and vitality because of self-acceptance at last. This has been Gail and Kay's experience because of their love for each other, sealed by the commitment ceremony they went ahead with even though their parents wouldn't attend. (Kay's grandmother attended, however.)

No heterosexual married couple could be more devoted than these two lesbians. And their commitment to Christ is strong and vibrant. Everyone notices the warmth and peaceful atmosphere of their home, the plaques and wall hangings declaring their faith, the music and laughter.

Kay and Gail have worked through many of their anxieties: the pain of knowing they are part of a stigmatized minority and cannot be open about the nature of their relationship, the struggle with self-acceptance (which still emerges in some form from time to time), the fear of losing their jobs because of ignorance and bigotry on the part of persons who don't understand homosexuality, the yearning for full acceptance by their families.

Gail and Kay wish more Christians would give serious
attention to the theological thinking many Christian
leaders are doing today, reexamining old ideas about
homosexuality and asking if the church hasn't made
some serious errors in its responsibility toward homosexual persons. The word "homosexual" does not appear in
the Bible; the concept of a basic orientation or *way of
being* was not even known. Same-sex *acts* in the context
of idolatry, rape (including gang rape), prostitution, lust-
ful promiscuity, and violation of ceremonial taboos were
condemned in biblical times—but so were sexual acts
between a man and a woman in such contexts. It appears
that the biblical writers were discussing neither the
homosexual *orientation* (a way of finding a same-sex
attraction more natural to oneself, just as a left-handed
person finds using the left hand more natural, even if the
majority of persons are right-handed) nor the possibility
of two homosexual persons joining their lives in a *committed monogamous relationship* and following the
same Christian ethic of faithfulness to which heterosexual married couples are enjoined. The Bible itself is
simply silent on these matters.

Yet Kay and Gail have sat in churches and heard
pastors condemn all homosexual persons to hell, saying
that as a group they have been "given up" by God. Using
parts of Romans 1 out of context, such pastors have
insisted that homosexual persons are ruled by perverted
lusts, are miserable, and have no love for God in their
hearts. They consider the notion of homosexual Christians to be a contradiction in terms. "These pastors
simply don't know gay persons as people," says Gail.
"They just think of stereotypes."

These women are glad that increasing numbers of
Christians are questioning the church's traditional attitudes toward homosexual persons—attitudes that so of-

ten have been harsh, judgmental, lacking in compassion, and uninformed by behavioral science research findings.

As Virginia Ramey Mollenkott and I point out in our book *Is the Homosexual My Neighbor?*, at the very least Christians owe it to lesbians and to homosexual men to include them in the neighbor love Jesus told us to show to all persons. That means not bearing false witness against our neighbor by asserting things that aren't true about homosexual persons. It means respecting their right as citizens to earn a living, to have a place to live, and to enjoy other civil rights. It means taking the time to study the topic (and, if possible, talking with homosexual persons who are open about their identity at least with a select group of friends), so that we can correct misinformation and help spread understanding. Many people are unaware that the American Psychiatric Association and the American Psychological Association no longer consider homosexuality a mental illness, because carefully conducted research in the social and behavioral sciences has convinced them otherwise. Similarly, many people are unaware of the various life-styles lived by homosexual persons. It is erroneous to think in terms of "*the* homosexual life-style," and especially erroneous if a promiscuous life-style is the first thing that comes to mind.

True, some gay persons do live promiscuously, just as do some heterosexual persons. But others live in committed, monogamous relationships and go about their lives and careers quietly and responsibly. Some gay men and lesbians live celibate lives, knowing they are attracted to the same sex but choosing not to act upon their sexual desires. And, as Gail and Kay have shown us, there are homosexual persons who are religiously devout and rest in an assurance that God created them, gave them their love, and accepts them just as they are. A concern for Christian love and justice calls us to be open, compas-

sionate, and understanding rather than to approach the
topic with the smug certainty that all the answers are
already in and we have the right to be judgmental and
self-righteous. We must be careful not to close our hearts
to what God may have to say to us through our homosexual sisters and brothers, who are our neighbors in the
biblical sense and for whom Christ died and rose again,
no less than for anyone else.

LONGINGS FOR INTIMACY

So often, what we think are sexual anxieties are really a
fear of being alone, of not having some special person in
our lives with whom we can relate at the deepest level of
our beings. Our longing is for intimacy, which comes
from the Latin word *intimus*, meaning "innermost,"
"deepest," "close friend."

Intimacy is not synonymous with sex—although, in
some cases, intimacy may include sexual relating. But
intimate relating doesn't have to be sexual relating. In
fact, sex in our day may be easier to find than intimacy.
Many people make the mistake of thinking that sex *is*
intimacy—or at least that sex is a shortcut to intimacy.
Then they wonder why the aching loneliness remains,
often hitting them even as they get up from the bed.
They have attempted a one-flesh relationship without
the experience of a one-soul relationship. In the next
chapter, we will explore the link between expressing our
sexuality and our quest for intimacy.

CHAPTER 6

Expressing Our Sexuality

Frederick II, a thirteenth-century emperor of Germany, wanted to find out what language children would grow up to speak if left entirely on their own. He wondered if the "natural" language of babies would turn out to be ancient Hebrew, Greek, or Latin; or would it be that of their birth parents, or what? The infants in his experiment were placed in the care of foster mothers and nurses who were to have minimal contact with them, attending only to their physical needs for food, bathing, and so on. The caretakers were forbidden to cuddle or rock the babies or speak to them or sing lullabies.

Frederick II never found the answers he sought through this strange experiment. All the babies died. "For they could not live without the petting and joyful faces and loving words of their foster mothers," explained a medieval historian. The story is recounted in anthropologist Ashley Montagu's informative book *Touching*, designed to help us more fully appreciate "the human significance of the skin."

THE HUMAN NEED FOR LOVE

Psychiatrist William Glasser, who pioneered the therapeutic method called "reality therapy," works from the
premise that human beings operate on the basis of two
primary psychological needs: (1) "the need to love and
be loved" and (2) "the need to feel that we are worthwhile to ourselves and to others" *(Reality Therapy,* p. 10).

According to Dr. Glasser, our sense of well-being is
associated with our acceptance of responsibility for
meeting these basic needs in the context of *reality*—the
world as it is, not as we might pretend it is or wish it to
be—and with sensitivity to others, who have these same
basic psychological needs to meet in their lives. Glasser
illustrates this point about responsibility by speaking of a
young woman who falls in love with a responsible man.
Such a man will either return the love she has for him
(fulfilling both their needs to give and to receive love) or
else he will tell her, with great care and consideration,
that he is grateful for her affection for him but does not
share the same feelings. On the other hand, if a man
learns of a woman's love for him and "takes advantage of
her love to gain some material or sexual end," says
Glasser, "we would not consider him responsible."

Borrowing from Glasser's framework, we might express his four major points in terms of four "R's" and
apply them usefully to the question of expressing oneself
sexually. A person facing a sexual decision could ask,
"Am I acting responsibly? Am I recognizing reality? Am
I relating lovingly and reciprocally so that I am both
giving and receiving love? Am I acting in a way that
enhances my respect for myself and helps to fulfill my
need to feel worthwhile as a human being?"

Marilyn, for example, is a twenty-eight-year-old secre-
tary who is very fearful that she'll never find someone to

marry. She has decided to be active sexually so that she at least will not "miss out" on that experience, and she often meets men at singles establishments. Yet she is haphazard about the use of contraceptive measures. She doesn't like the Pill because it affects her weight. She is careless in using her diaphragm consistently because she feels it interferes with romantic moments and also makes her appear prepared for sexual intercourse with a man she hardly knows—which goes against the "nice girl" image she holds of herself. Sometimes a man will tell her he has had a vasectomy and she trustingly takes him at his word, pushing any concern about contraceptive precautions from her mind. Marilyn is not acting responsibly.

Or take Sandy. For thirteen years, Sandy has been secretly having an affair with Bill, a married man. He keeps telling her just to be patient and "give him time," that he really cares about her and that "someday," when things settle down in his career and family, he will divorce his wife and marry Sandy. All the evidence indicates that "someday" isn't likely to come. Meanwhile, Sandy's life is on hold. Even apart from the moral issue of participating in an adulterous relationship, Sandy needs to wake up to the fact that by continuing this arrangement she is not recognizing reality.

Sandy is afraid to recognize that the relationship is basically one-sided. She gives freely of her love, time, energy, and money, and Bill takes full advantage of her, giving her little in return except occasional sex when it suits his fancy and fits his schedule (and then she is expected to drop everything and meet him right away). She is also losing respect for herself. She wants to believe that having him in her life makes her feel loved and worthwhile. But it isn't working out that way.

Responsible people don't use other people. They don't lay the responsibility for their sexual longings onto other people. They realize their own responsibility for fulfilling personal needs for love and positive self-esteem in ways that are sensitive to the similar needs of others and that respect their wishes, convictions, and overall well-being. Persons who handle their sexual longings responsibly don't pressure other people or manipulate them by playing on softheartedness or guilt feelings. Many single people are familiar with lines like these from the teenage years onward: "If you won't have sex with me, it proves you don't really love me. You just care about yourself." Or "I need sexual relief. You don't want me to suffer, do you?" Or even "What a frigid woman you are!" We usually are familiar with male sex lines, but there are female lines, too. One young woman told a man she needed sexual intercourse as a "medical treatment" to help relieve her tendency to have severe menstrual cramps monthly!

What many people call sexual "needs" are not really needs in the same sense as the need for food, water, and air to breathe. They may be sexual *wants*, but they aren't needs in the strictest sense of the word. No one has ever died for lack of sexual expression. Realizing this distinction between need and desire can be freeing for the person who has felt driven by sexual urges. The drivenness need no longer control such persons, or propel them into situations that are not in their own best interest.

Paul addressed this same issue when writing to the Corinthian Christians. They lived in a city famed for sexual looseness; and upon their conversion to Christ, many of the Corinthians' overzealousness for freedom in Christ led them to embrace an "anything goes" attitude toward sexual expression—including having sex with prostitutes. They argued, "All things are lawful for me!" And Paul countered, "Yes, but not all things are helpful." They tried again, reminding him of the doctrine of Christian liberty, "All things are lawful for me." And

Paul acknowledged this was true but pointed out that some behavior can be enslaving, putting us under its control. "I will not be enslaved by anything," he said.

And then they used a "sex is a natural, physical need" approach. "Food is meant for the stomach and the stomach for food," they argued. In other words, if an appetite exists, what's wrong with gratifying it? Paul pointed out that the digestive system with its need for sustenance was representative of the temporal, biological cravings of earthly existence. The day would come when the stomach and its need for nourishment would no longer exist. The body, in contrast, would live on forever. The body, as Paul was speaking of it, was to be considered much more than the sum of its transitory parts. He wanted us to see the body in terms of our permanent individuality or personhood, the temple of the Holy Spirit, designed to glorify God and destined for resurrection. Sexuality must be seen as part of the body in *this* sense rather than simply in the biological sense. Paul wanted Christians to understand that, when viewed this way, "the body is not meant for immorality, but for the Lord, and the Lord for the body." (See I Cor. 6:12–20.)

In this passage, Paul again alluded to the ideal of the one-flesh relationship that cannot be experienced as anything but a travesty or farce when it is attempted in casual, promiscuous sexual encounters. The one-flesh ideal in the context of a loving covenant, as we saw in Chapters 3 and 4, emphasizes sexual intimacy in a relationship of overall intimacy.

Intimacy, as Mary Calderone and Eric Johnson point out in *The Family Book About Sexuality,* requires a number of basic ingredients: *time, mutual desire for closeness, reciprocity* (equal commitment, with both persons equally investing in the relationship), and *trust* (with both parties opening up to each other and being vulnerable to each other). Calderone and Johnson point out that the growing sense of safety in revealing one's inner self that comes with trust leads to the ultimate expression: "free and open delight one in the other." Calderone and Johnson conclude:

> And this, to us, has to be the ultimate meaning of the word *intimacy*, for when two people delight each other, and delight in each other, in an atmosphere of security based on mutuality, reciprocity, and total trust each in the other, whatever their age or sex or relationship, this is surely the kind of relationship that every human being seeks, even if it does not involve physical sex (p. 32).

So many people are searching for such intimacy in the wrong way. They expect genital sexual connecting to provide instant intimacy in the manner of instant coffee or instant photos. They are reaching out for *love*. And love, rather than sex, as we saw in the beginning of this chapter, *is* a basic, human psychological need. So is human touch.

THE HUMAN NEED FOR BODY CONTACT

Ashley Montagu has pointed out that "in the Western world it is highly probable that sexual activity, indeed the frenetic preoccupation with sex that characterizes Western culture, is in many cases not the expression of a sexual interest at all, but rather a search for the satisfaction of the need for contact" (*Touching*, p. 166). He cites the studies of several behavioral scientists who found that women who had sometimes been labeled "oversexed" because of their desperate pursuit of sexual experiences were in reality women who were simply starved for skin contact. The physical ache these women described was not related to erotic excitement and a desire for orgasmic release at all; rather, it stemmed from unsatisfied needs for touching, holding, and cuddling that had gone unmet from infancy onward. They thought the only acceptable way to get such holding was through genital sexual expression, so that's what they offered men.

One director of a Christian home for unwed mothers points out that the adolescent women who come there have by and large turned to sexual experimentation out of a frantic longing to be held. A considerable number of the teenagers come from rigidly religious families where, in the parents' minds, touching, hugging, and holding are associated with sex; and such expressions are restrained or virtually nonexistent as the children are growing up. At puberty, sexual activities appear to be a way to get the cuddling that was missing in family life. A number of sexuality educators concur with this observation that what is commonly decried as "irresponsible teenage promiscuity" can in many cases be traced to a gnawing hunger for love and holding.

In the early part of this century, physicians were puzzled and alarmed by the mortality rate of infants in orphanages. Rarely did a child reach his or her second birthday. The small percentage who did were babies who were taken out of the orphanages for brief stays in foster homes. It was thought that the babies were prone to a rare disease; they were simply "wasting away" and dying without explanation—in spite of the finest medical care and efforts at good nutrition. Only gradually did medical experts come to see that what was killing the babies was emotional starvation and the lack of tender, loving care through holding, rocking, and cuddling— much as had happened in Frederick II's "baby language" experiment seven centuries earlier. It is now known that skin stimulation is a crucial need in infancy, and its lack can cause all sorts of developmental and emotional problems later in life.

"In children who are receiving lots of skin hunger care and comfort I can see clear eyes and an energy which seems to flow directly and effortlessly through their bodies," writes educator Sidney Simon. He continues:

> I feel that I can always tell a child who is well touched—the one with the bright eyes who looks out at the world openly and unafraid. There are, of course, the furtive eyes of those who do not get touched at all, or the glassy eyes of those who get touched a lot but only for purposes of sex. The difference, as I said, is easily discerned by a teacher.
>
> *(Caring, Feeling, Touching,* pp. 26–27)

Leo Buscaglia, known for his enthusiastic lectures and books and his course on love at the University of Southern California, tells in his book *Living, Loving, and Learning* of growing up in a large, warm, Italian immigrant family where hugs and kisses were the order of the day and the taboo against touching was unknown. One day, his teacher sent a note home saying the boy was "too tactile." His mother, not yet fluent in English and troubled to receive this first note from an American teacher, asked him what "tactile" meant. The boy said he honestly didn't know what the word meant or what he had done. Looking up the word in the dictionary, the family found it related to feeling and touching. Buscaglia reports that his mother asked what was wrong with that; she considered touching a nice thing to do. "You got a crazy teacher," she concluded (p. 229).

Buscaglia's contagious enthusiasm for nonerotic hugging and touching is part of a growing interest in the human need for skin contact. We see it in the baby massage movement, the therapeutic touch movement in the nursing profession, or in the ministry of someone like Mother Teresa of India as she and her co-workers embody God's love through touching with compassion and comfort the poor, the sick, the dying, the lonely, and the despairing.

Helen Colton, in her book *The Gift of Touch,* suggests that one reason so many young people have been drawn to the various cults in recent years is that the cults offer something missing in their own families in many cases—hugging, holding, touching, and caring. Colton also wonders if some problems of obesity in adult life might not relate to a childhood association of food with comfort and affection. Often it is the child's *skin,* not her or his tummy, that is hungry. The child seeks a hug and instead is given a piece of candy or a cracker and told to run off and play. For some women, food becomes a substitute for the embracing and caressing they long for in adult life as well, regardless of their marital status. Montagu, in his study of the human need for touching, refers to another problem, one seen in dermatologists' offices on occasion. "The various forms of psychosomatic pruritus—that is, functionally induced itching of the skin—often represent the unconscious striving to obtain the attention that was denied in early life, especially the attention that was denied to the skin," he writes *(Touching,* p. 151*).*

Jesus was well aware of the touch needs of people. As we look through the Gospels we notice again and again that he reached out to touch people and allowed them to touch him—babies and children, people unable to see or hear or walk, persons afflicted with all manner of diseases, a woman who was ceremonially unclean under the law because of her unending menstrual discharge, the Roman soldier whose ear Peter cut off as Jesus was arrested, the beloved disciple who rested his head against Jesus in the upper room.

Perhaps Jesus' openness to touch is nowhere more clear than in the incident described in Luke 7:36–50. Gratefully and graciously, Jesus accepted the devotion of a woman who came off the streets and washed his feet with her tears, dried them with her hair, kissed them, and anointed them with an expensive ointment. His dinner host, a proper Pharisee who prided himself on respectability, was shocked. A prostitute coming to his dinner table, and Jesus putting up with it? How could Jesus possibly be a prophet of God and let himself be touched by such a person? And in such an intimate way! Didn't he know what sort of woman she was? What would people think? Simon, the Pharisee, probably shuddered in revulsion.

Jesus knew what Simon was thinking. He reminded Simon that *he* hadn't bothered to greet Jesus warmly and affectionately, nor did he perform the footwashing duties of a thoughtful host in that culture. "I came into your home, and you gave me no water for my feet," Jesus said, "but she has washed my feet with her tears and dried them with her hair. You did not welcome me with a kiss, but she has not stopped kissing my feet since I came. You provided no olive oil for my head, but she has covered my feet with perfume. I tell you, then, the great love she has shown proves that her many sins have been forgiven" (Luke 7:44–47, TEV).

Think how that woman must have felt at that moment! Jesus was affirming her personhood by appreciating her gift of touch. She saw herself reflected in his eyes as someone of worth and dignity, someone with something to contribute. She had given the unusual gift of a foot massage, and Jesus had accepted it as the gift of love that it was. He treated her as a person of value. Probably she had never been regarded that way before. And her life would never be the same again. The power of loving touch works both ways, so that each person is both receiver and giver.

"When I give a massage, I find it's energy restoring for me as well as for the other person," a licensed masseuse told me recently. A nurse by profession and a deeply devoted follower of Christ, she says she studied the art of massage as a way she could give of herself to other people. She looks upon it as a ministry, a "different kind of therapy," a way of helping handle stress and the pressures of modern life. She is well aware that the idea of a massage is "scary, if touch is associated with sexuality" and speaks of the need for trust and care to assure a person that erotic touch will not be used. She tells of elderly people who have burst into tears upon being massaged; the experience of human touch provides them with such a release of tension and such a source of comfort. "Single older people often go for months without ever being touched," this woman says sadly. (This need for skin contact among the elderly is increasingly being recognized today; one effort to help fulfill it has been the introduction of pets into some nursing homes, providing a living creature for stroking and cuddling, thus resulting in a tremendous uplift of morale.)

Perhaps at this point you are wondering what all this emphasis on touch has to do with the title of this chapter, "Expressing Our Sexuality." I believe it has a great deal to do with it, because I think it can help us see some options we might have overlooked before.

In *Sex Is a Parent Affair* I pointed out four functions of human sexual expression that are forthrightly recognized in the Bible: *procreation, recreation* (the joy and fun aspect that we saw in the Song of Solomon), *communication* (the exchange of affection, a conversation of love that is beyond language, the reason perhaps that sexual intercourse in Scripture is often spoken of as "knowing"), and *orgasmic release* (which Paul was acknowledging in his reference to "burning" with sexual desire in I Cor. 7:9). All these functions can be a wonderful part of marriage.

But for the woman alone—never married, or divorced,

or widowed, or perhaps with a severely incapacitated spouse (for example, from a stroke) whose illness makes even the creative sexual expression possibilities for disabled persons out of the question—must all sexual expression be denied? Some women say absolutely not and have sought to fulfill any or all of the four functions just mentioned without seeking commitment from their partner or partners, being content to be sexual "freelancers."

Other women believe this answer would violate their religious convictions and don't feel comfortable with such a solution. They are persuaded that the full expression of erotic, genital sexuality with another person is to be reserved for the covenantal bond that marriage was intended to represent.

However, sexual desires and the longings for intimacy and human touch may be met in other ways. For example, masturbation is a satisfactory way of achieving the sexual pleasure of orgasmic release—a way of "making love to yourself," which many women find solves the erotic stirrings that arise from time to time. The Scriptures say absolutely nothing about the practice, and there is no reason to think it's "evil" behavior if one has a healthy attitude toward sex. Some Christian leaders have suggested that masturbation might be a gift provided by God so that persons can enjoy their sexuality even though they are not in a partnership.

As for needs for human touch and intimacy, the development of deep, close, one-soul friendships with persons of the same sex and of the opposite sex may be the means of fulfilling such needs. Hugs, holding, stroking the hair, giving back rubs—all these ways and more can be means of nourishment at the deepest levels of our being. What is an appropriate level of affection or type of affectionate expression depends upon the particular relationship and must be decided by the persons involved. Open communication is crucial—particularly if there is a fear that the comforting, caring touch boundaries are being crossed or are blurring into the erotic in a way that makes anyone uneasy.

Basically, most persons' fear of touch springs from associating all touch with erotic touch. Barbara Roberts, a therapist and director of the Center for Social and Sensory Learning in Tarzana, California, has made a list of the consequences of certain beliefs about touch. For example, if we believe that *any* touching can arouse someone sexually, we may conclude that *no* touch is permissible unless it is for the express purpose of sexual arousal. The only exceptions, in this way of thinking, are the touch we are permitted to give if someone is in physical or emotional pain or the touching permitted for children or old people. According to Roberts, the consequences of such beliefs include giving affectional touch "only as a prelude to sex," denying the human need for physical closeness for its own sake, hindering real intimacy, and substituting sex for emotional closeness. Persons with touch taboos bring to a relationship the suspicion "that all touch is either a sexual invitation or that sexual feelings will be aroused inappropriately," Roberts stated in a meeting of the Society for the Scientific Study of Sex (reported in *Sexuality Today,* Aug. 22, 1983, p. 3).

Many women who feel sexually deprived are actually *sensually* deprived—starved for touch, needing skin contact. If we women can put aside our fears of sex, we can bring much nurture to one another. The masseuse I mentioned earlier suggested the benefits that could be derived from a weekly massage from someone in whom one could feel complete trust. Simple, nonthreatening touching exercises such as those given in Simon's *Caring, Feeling, Touching* can be useful too. (He especially recommends these exercises for parents and children.)

Gloria Steinem, in the article mentioned in the preced-

ing chapter, told of meeting a masseuse who massaged
the pain from an elderly woman's arthritic hands, helped
drain the tension from persons whose necks and backs
were knotted with tension, helped stressful people find
sleep without taking pills. "With unselfconscious pride,
she contemplates a career of easing the bodies of tired
women," Steinem writes. "We agree that, if everyone
had one good massage a day, there would be fewer wars"
(*Ms. Magazine*, April 1982, p. 31, used by permission).

Perhaps she has a point.

CHAPTER 7

Our Sexual Hurts

Many women carry in their hearts great pain from sexual hurts. And often they feel all alone. It is hard to talk about such matters, and even finding an empathic listener can be difficult.

In recent years, with more public awareness of incest, rape, sexual harassment, and other sexual abuses, support groups have sprung up to help guide women through the anguish that is such a part of sexual hurts— whether they are hurts from recent events or are the deeply scarred memories of hurts from long ago. Women need to hear one another and comfort and help bring healing to one another. In a sexual hurt such as rape or the sexual abuse of a child, not only the person's body has been violated; the innermost spirit and sense of personhood feels the pain as well.

RAPE

She was a university sophomore. He was a senior, planning to attend a theological seminary the following year. They had gone out together three or four times before—had enjoyed talking and laughing over a pizza at a restaurant near campus, had gone to a movie, and had

nded a church service and Bible study together. They
d seriously discussed their future career plans and
their Christian faith. Everything about the relationship
seemed positive and promising and gave no hint of what
was coming.

Then one evening he invited her up to his room to see
his stereo equipment and record collection. She saw no
reason not to go; he was someone she knew and trusted.
In the room he turned on the stereo loudly, locked the
door with a dead-bolt lock and key, threw her down on
his bed, and raped her.

When he released her, his face was full of contempt for
her. She was stunned and frightened but somehow found
her way to the campus health services building. She told
the staff what had happened and was given a "morning-
after" pill as a precaution against possible pregnancy.
She did not report the incident to the police. The shock
and agonizing hurt did not heal easily or quickly.

Unfortunately, this young woman's story is more common than most of us realize. The phenomenon of "date
rape" or "acquaintance rape" is not the hushed-up subject it once was. Some rape counselors are in fact warning
young women that rapes are more likely to occur on a
date with someone they know than with a stranger who
assaults them at some unguarded moment. One young
college woman was even raped by a fellow student who
expressed concern about her walking home alone late at
night and offered to walk with her, winning her trust and
then trampling on it.

This betrayal of trust is one of the most excruciating
aspects of acquaintance rape. There may also be a great
deal of self-blame (which, sadly, is reinforced by society's tendency to "blame the victim" in rape cases). The
woman may wonder if she lacks good judgment of
character or if there was something about her (her manner, the way she was dressed, something she said?) that

caused such a thing to happen. Her religious faith may be shaken as she wonders why God didn't protect her. She may feel abandoned by her peers as well; some of them simply don't know what to say or how to comfort her, while others imply that she was somehow at fault and shouldn't have let herself get into such a situation. Or they may imply that she wasn't really raped but rather consented in some way.

Marie Fortune, an ordained minister who directs the Center for the Prevention of Sexual and Domestic Violence in Seattle, Washington, stresses the need to recognize the distinction between sexual violence and sexual activity and to see that sexual violence is *not* simply an extreme form of sexual activity; it is in a wholly different category. The key word is not *sexual* but *violence.* It is an issue not of free choice but of coercion—force.

That's the point that is often overlooked in the emotional aftermath of rape, as insensitive people look at the rape victim strangely and ask questions about what the experience was like. All that such people can think about is the young woman's "changed status," because their minds hold only an "unopened-package" view of virginity. They cannot grasp the truth that "God looks on the heart," not the broken hymen, and knows that the woman was robbed and battered no less than the traveler who was mugged by thieves on the road to Jericho and was rescued by the good Samaritan. That is why, over the ages, persons living close to the heart of God have emphasized that a virginal woman who is raped is still a virgin in God's eyes. There is absolutely no excuse for the reprehensible behavior of two Fundamentalist young men who went to a Christian student after a rapist had climbed through a window of her apartment and attacked her. They told her that no Christian man would ever want to marry her now, because she was no longer a virgin. Their callousness and cruelty so added to her pain that she quit college and moved back home.

Marie Fortune underscores the nature of sexual violence and how totally it violates the person:

> During the attack or the abuse, the victim is not only out of control of her/his situation, but the victim is also assaulted in the most vulnerable dimension of the self. A sexual attack makes it clear that something has been taken away. Power has been taken away. The power to decide, to choose, to determine, to consent or withhold consent in the most concrete bodily dimension, all vanish in the face of the rapist or child molester. Being forced sexually against one's will is the ultimate experience of powerlessness, short of death.
>
> *(Sexual Violence: The Unmentionable Sin, pp. 6–7)*

The sense of powerlessness and betrayal can seem unbearable when the rapist is one's own husband. One woman shared with me the journal account she wrote describing the first time her husband raped her. They were at a motel, celebrating their first anniversary, when he forced open the bathroom door and announced, "I'm gonna have some fun tonight. I'm gonna rape you!" She recalled he had said the same thing on the drive to the motel. She continued to get dressed to go out for the evening as they had planned and tried to dismiss his remarks as a strange attempt at humor.

Suddenly her husband lunged toward her and began punching her, ripping off her clothing violently, slapping her in the face, and pushing her onto the motel bed. He locked his knee into her abdomen and held her arms together over her head with one hand as he took off his own clothes with his other hand. When she resisted, he pounded her more fiercely and bit her face and breasts. Finally, the rape was over. The woman herself continues the story:

I was bewildered and felt so violated, while my husband "assured" me of his love and devotion. He said he was "just playing" and it wouldn't happen again. That violent one-act play, with the beating and raping, was performed in a multitude of versions during the next two years until the day I took all the pills [in a suicide attempt that almost succeeded].

(From the woman's personal diary.
Used by permission. All rights reserved.)

The woman had tried again and again to get help during that two-year period—from members of the clergy, marriage counselors, a close friend, and a physician. But no one would believe her story. The couple was known as a model couple in their church, and the husband was considered a gentle, quiet Christian man. Only the suicide attempt and the husband's attack on the woman as she recovered in the hospital—an attack witnessed by a social worker who walked into the room at that point—convinced others of the truth of her story.

Unpleasant truth is hard to acknowledge. The same thing happens in cases of child molestation—especially when the molester is a person known and loved. Some persons find it easier to deny reality and to believe that a child or a wife made up stories of what happened than to confront the ugly truth. Such attitudes perpetuate sexual abuse by looking the other way and can add untold suffering to victims by making them doubt their own experience after a time. The victims may even wonder about their own sanity.

Wife rape takes place primarily because of the imbalance of power inherent in traditional male and female roles, along with attitudes and societal expectations that tacitly give men permission to behave violently and aggressively and to be characterized by "predatory sexuality." This is the conclusion of sociologist Diana Russell after conducting a massive study of marital rape. "Wife rape is equally a manifestation of a male sexuality which is oriented to conquest and domination," writes Russell, "and to proving masculinity." She goes on to show the problems that come from defining masculinity in terms of superiority, control, power, and aggressiveness. In this way of thinking, "a 'real man' is supposed to get what he wants, when he wants, particularly with his wife, and even more particularly in his sexual relations with her," writes Russell (*Rape in Marriage*, p. 357).

It was such an attitude that prompted a California state senator in 1979 to reply to women lobbying for changes in rape laws, "But if you can't rape your wife, who can you rape?" (quoted in Russell, p. 18). And it is a sense of powerlessness in the face of such attitudes that keeps some women feeling trapped in marriages where they are raped and beaten. Not only do many feel trapped by economic dependence; some wives have actually been told by religious leaders that their husbands have a "right" to do what they want to the women's bodies because a wife's body belongs to her husband. (This is a gross misapplication of I Cor. 7:4, where, as we have seen, mutuality and equality in the husband-wife sex relationship are stressed.)

A conquest attitude toward women—the "predatory sexuality" that Russell talks about—also characterizes men who participate in gang rapes, whether carried out by fraternity men who try to laugh it off as a "boys will be boys" college prank or by men in vastly different circumstances. Such incidents spring from a contempt for women and carry to the extreme a belief that some men extract from male socialization: the belief that women exist for the service and pleasure of men and that males have the right to rule over females and objectify them as nonpersons. A horrible illustration of this attitude is seen in one of the Bible's most gruesome stories, the story of the gang rape in Judges 19.

Rape is not a crime of passion but of power—power in which sex is used as a weapon for hurting, humiliating, frightening, and conquering another person, *forcing* submission to the rapist's will.

SEXUAL ABUSE OF CHILDREN

Power is also involved when an adult involves a child in sexual activities. The power differentiation involves differences in size, life experience, knowledge of what sexual activity means, dependency, and authority status. An ideology of male superiority, sometimes religiously based and fortified by a misuse and abuse of Bible passages, is also found in some cases of father-daughter incest. In the most extreme example I have read about, one father actually had a throne set up in his house and required his three daughters to perform sexual acts with him. This case is recorded in a collection of readings published by the National Center on Child Abuse and Neglect (p. 55). The same publication provides the Center's definition of child sexual abuse, which consists of "contacts or interactions between a child and an adult when the child is being used as an object of gratification for adult sexual needs or desires" (*Sexual Abuse of Children*, p. 1). Approximately one half to three quarters or more of incidences of the sexual abuse of children involve somebody the child knows and trusts—a father or father figure, brother, uncle, grandfather, cousin, teacher, club leader, camp counselor, religious leader, and so on. Most such sexual encounters are coercive without being violent in the sense of causing major *physical* injuries—though these of course occur and can cause serious vaginal tearing and anal injuries, as well as transmission of venereal diseases. The emotional and psychological damage is another matter.

Child sexual abuse may involve exhibitionism, fondling the child's genitals or asking the child to fondle the offender's genitals or perform oral sex with him. Or it may involve actual vaginal or anal intercourse—the size difference alone in such cases raising the potential for pain and injury, especially in young children.

When children are drawn into sexual activities and "sexual games" with trusted adults, physical force is not usually used—though the threat of it may be employed in some cases. ("If you tell anyone our special little secret, you'll be punished!" or "You'd better do as I say or you're going to be in trouble!") More often, other forms of coercion or bribery are used. The child is told that he or she will be given some special gift for doing what the adult wants or that this is a way to show love to the adult. If the child hesitates and doesn't feel good about participating, the adult may misrepresent moral standards and assure the child that nothing is wrong with such behavior and that everybody does it. The child's innocence is exploited, and the adult takes full advantage of his position of power and dominance. (The male pronoun is intentional; child sexual abuse by adult females is extremely rare. Regardless of the sex of the abused child, the offender is almost always a male.)

Women who were victims of father-daughter incest during childhood and early adolescence are a special category of women suffering from sexual hurts. For years, these women have kept locked in their hearts a secret that haunts and shames them. And they have a vague sense of something hanging over them, something unresolved, something requiring some sort of action—but they're not sure what. They feel confusion, guilt, anger, and a longing for relief from painful memories that have resurfaced in dreams and other ways even when they have attempted to suppress or deny them. They may experience psychological by-products of the sexual trauma they experienced, including difficulties in adult relationships, often extending even to mistrust of therapists they consult.

Addressing this issue, psychiatrist Judith Lewis Herman suggests that a therapist first help the client recognize that she has difficulty in intimate relationships and then help her see that "this difficulty stems in large part from her inability to feel trust when trust is appropriate and, conversely, to protect herself when trust is not appropriate; and third, that this problem is almost certainly related to her history of having been abused and neglected by her parents." Recognizing this at the outset helps the therapist and client work together on any reactions the client might have while defusing "the whole issue of complicity and blame," Herman points out. "The therapist makes it clear to the patient that regardless of her behavior, the fact that she was involved in incest as a child means that she could not have been properly cared for." The therapy can then be focused on the consequence of such improper care: the woman's difficulties in adult intimate relationships *(Father-Daughter Incest,* p. 190).

Sometimes even trust in a therapist or religious counselor turns out to have been misplaced, and the incest victim is exploited and hurt all over again by a powerful male authority figure. In recent years, public attention has been drawn to the minority of therapists and members of the clergy who breach professional ethics by taking advantage of their clients and engaging them in sexual activities. Herman points out that the incest victim's feelings of shame and guilt are relived in such instances and "the result is a calamitous repetition of the original incest." The woman's early experiences impressed on her that "no man can possibly care for her without a sexual relationship"; and, having low self-esteem and longing for affection, she may not feel sexual involvement is "too high a price to have to pay for the therapist's attention." Herman continues:

> Once entrapped in a sexual relationship with a therapist, the patient relives the betrayal and disappointment that she first experienced with her father. The outcome can only be a disaster for her. To add insult to injury, the therapist usually rationalizes the sexual relationship as an attempt to help the patient with her problems, thus requiring her to feel grateful.
>
> *(Father-Daughter Incest, p. 187)*

THE HEALING OF SEXUAL HURTS

Persons who have undergone sexual trauma such as rape and incest need to have their self-worth affirmed and to be assured that they are not to blame. Something sexual has been *done to* them, forced on them; it was not something they willingly chose or participated in. Even if there is some appearance of consent and guilt over that compliance—for example, ongoing sexual activities with a father over a period of years—the power issue has to be stressed. The blame lies with the caretaker who misused his power and position.

Victims of sexual abuse need opportunities to vent their feelings and fears in a safe, supportive environment. Rape crisis centers can be helpful in providing counseling and literature. Marie Fortune's book *Sexual Violence* has excellent material on pastoral counseling in situations of sexual abuse. For women who have been incest victims, support groups have proven especially helpful. In such groups, women can begin to feel less alone and to gain perspective on what was done to them. They are able to resolve confusion about certain behaviors, as they find that there are common patterns in incest. (For example, they may hear other women talk about how strict and religious their fathers were, how those fathers didn't want their daughters to date, how they warned constantly about sexual promiscuity and yet justified their own sexual activities with their daughters; or they may hear of fathers who treated their daughters as "little wives," with major housekeeping responsibilities, while the mothers were ill or were employed outside the home.) Many women find new strength as well as relief and self-acceptance in such groups, and they may mobilize that strength to help others through educational and intervention work through women's centers and other community efforts to help women and children in crisis.

There *is* hope for those who know the pain of sexual hurt—those discussed here and any other hurt. "[God] heals the broken-hearted, and bandages their wounds." (Ps. 147:3, TEV.) God goes through our suffering with us and brings us to new life and hope on the other side of pain.

CHAPTER 8

Sexuality
Over Our Life Span

A baby snuggles against the mother's breast, tiny lips wrapped around her nipple drawing nourishment. The mother smiles as she tenderly traces a finger against the infant's soft cheek. Both feel a cozy warmth and contentment. They are at one.

The scene describes a sensuous experience, an awareness of the joy and mystery of life by way of the *senses* God has given us. Enjoyment of the sense of touch is especially predominant here and lays the groundwork for the infant's sexual relating later on in her or his lifetime.

But the mother, too, is experiencing sensuous pleasure and an awareness of deep bonding. Some breast-feeding mothers may be shocked to realize that sometimes they also experience actual sexual arousal during nursing, and they may think of such feelings as bad and inappropriate and try to deny them. They need reassurance that such feelings are perfectly normal and are in fact triggered by a natural physiological response to a certain hormone involved in lactation. Such feelings have nothing to do with incest proclivities such as were discussed in the preceding chapter!

CHILDHOOD AND PUBERTY

The old saying "More is caught than taught" certainly applies to the transmission of sexual attitudes and values. Infants and small children are learning a positive attitude toward sexuality in their earliest years as their parents help them build a sense of self-worth and an appreciation of their bodies as wonderful creations of God. The experience of being cuddled and hugged and observing their parents' love for each other provides the best possible atmosphere for gradual sexual learning.

In such an atmosphere of love and trust, parents can convey their openness to the questions of their growing children. And they can initiate conversations themselves by taking advantage of all kinds of sex education opportunities in everyday family life. A pet dog's pregnancy, a newspaper article about test-tube babies, a child's discovery of a box of sanitary napkins, and a television program about teenage pregnancy or sexually transmitted diseases can all serve as discussion springboards for alert parents.

Today's children are by no means sheltered, and parents are only fooling themselves if they think their children are not being exposed to sexual information in one form or another. Parents have the unique opportunity of being their children's first and primary sex educators, helping their children learn to think for themselves in the sexual decisions they will face throughout life. Sex education has two sides—the teaching of facts and the teaching of values—and parents can help their children to integrate biological information with moral guidance based on the children's personal religious faith. A number of sexuality education books have been written especially for parents in recent years to aid them in their task. A few you might wish to consider are *The Family*

Book About Sexuality by Mary Calderone and Eric
Johnson, *Raising a Child Conservatively in a Sexually
Permissive World* by Sol Gordon and Judith Gordon, and
my own *Sex Is a Parent Affair*, which is designed for the
Christian home and written for the parent who is looking
for a biblically based approach to sexuality education.
Each of these books is written in a warm, personal tone
and popular style and is full of practical help.

As puberty approaches and we see our children entering young adulthood, new challenges present themselves both to us and to our children. Menstruation,
nocturnal emissions, growth of pubic hair, breast development, voice changes, and changes in the genitals all
signal that the bodies of our daughters and sons are
preparing for their reproductive functions. It's important
to show great sensitivity to our children at this stage,
remembering our own adolescent feelings and how
strange our once familiar bodies seemed as they underwent so many changes. Interest in sexual matters is
increasing at this stage (God programmed human bodies
that way), and parents who have encouraged open communication and nonjudgmentalism all along can continue to help their teenagers make wise, ethical decisions
about how they handle their sexuality.

ADULT YEARS: THE MARRIED WOMAN

Women who grew up in homes where communication
about sexuality was not open and positive often have
difficulty with sex in marriage. They can't seem to give
themselves permission to let go, relax, and enjoy. The
old scripts keep going around in their heads like a
recording: "Sex is dirty." "Nice girls don't enjoy sex."
"It's animal-like to let go of my inhibitions the way he
wants me to. If I did, he'd never respect me afterward."
"My parents would be *shocked* if they knew he wanted

me to try oral sex. This isn't right! I was brought up differently. I feel cheap."

Sex *role* scripts especially—those messages that tell us what a male or a female is "supposed" to do and feel—can stifle pleasure and spontaneity in the marriage bed and elsewhere in the relationship. Traditional sex roles block emotional intimacy. Part of the problem is the attachment–autonomy split. Women are socialized to put great stress on attachment—being close to someone, pleasing others, valuing relationships. They are encouraged to feel deeply and to express their feelings freely through words, tears, tender touches, and other ways. Thus women have little difficulty experiencing deep emotional intimacy in their friendships with one another—a fact noticed by a considerable number of men today who have begun vocalizing their envy of female friendships.

Male friendships tend to be characterized by emotional distance and guardedness. Men have been socialized *not* to feel deeply—as though human feeling must stand opposed to rationality—and they have been discouraged from letting any feelings show. "Big boys are brave; they don't cry. Only girls and sissies cry." *Talking* about deep feelings doesn't come easily either; males don't want to be vulnerable. In other words, while women have been taught to stress the importance of *attachment*, men have been taught that *autonomy* is what matters—being independent, self-sufficient, goal oriented, and emotionally restrained (except for explosions of anger and the socially permitted exuberant discharge of emotions over sporting events).

When the two sexes get together, working at intimacy can be difficult; so many barriers of divergent socialization must be overcome. While the wife may yearn for and expect emotional intimacy with her husband comparable to what she enjoys with her women friends, her husband may be puzzled over her discontent. *He* is probably gaining from her emotional stroking and sharing at a depth he has never known in male friendships. Everything seems fine to him. He may criticize his wife for being "too dependent" or "too demanding" when she expresses a desire for more emotional sharing on his part. Many couples today are working to bring the attachment–autonomy issue into balance and to overcome traditional sex role socialization.

Freedom from traditional sex role scripts is especially important in the sexual relationship of a couple. Such freedom is abundantly clear in the Song of Solomon, as we saw earlier. In that book both persons freely gave and freely received, without either one feeling that certain actions were reserved for one sex or the other and that one must "act out a part" rather than spontaneously express love as seemed best for the individual. This kind of ideal lovemaking is described by Abraham Maslow in his classic psychological work on "self-actualizing persons"—that is, persons open to the development of their full potential as human beings. In the area of sexuality, Maslow found that such people "made no really sharp differentiation between the roles and personalities of the sexes." He writes:

> That is, they did not assume that the female was passive and the male active, whether in sex or love or anything else. These people were all so certain of their maleness or femaleness that they did not mind taking on some of the cultural aspects of the opposite sex role. It was especially noteworthy that they could be both active and passive lovers and this was clearest in the sexual act and in physical lovemaking. Kissing and being kissed, being above or below in the sexual act, taking the initiative, being

quiet and receiving love, teasing and being
teased—these were all found in both sexes.
(Motivation and Personality, p. 189)

As couples become more open and flexible in gender
roles and put genuine effort into developing greater
emotional intimacy, they are likely to find more mutually
satisfactory solutions to other sexuality issues that arise—
for example, frequency of sexual intercourse, techniques
of lovemaking, and reproductive concerns (such as infer-
tility problems, on the one hand, or decisions about
contraceptive methods, including sterilization, on the
other), to name just a few.

ADULT YEARS: THE WOMAN ALONE

"But what if there's nobody to celebrate your sexuality
with?" The question was asked by a widow in early
middle age as she flipped through a copy of Dwight
Small's book, *Christian: Celebrate Your Sexuality,* lying
on my desk.

Her question is asked by many women who have never
married or who have entered the "single again" category
through divorce or the death of a spouse. The usual
answers are three: (1) you don't celebrate your sexuality
at all, you bury it; (2) you find a partner for sexual
expression outside marriage; or (3) you get married or
remarried.

But there's a fourth possibility: Celebrate your sexuality yourself! No, that doesn't mean that one becomes an
isolated, self-centered recluse, obsessed with fantasies
and masturbation. (Although, as we saw in Chapter 6,
masturbation can be an excellent way of relieving sexual
tension and enjoying one's own body in a positive
celebration of God's gift of sex.)

I'm thinking of something broader here, a broader concept of what sexuality is all about. Going beyond the genital expression of sexuality, we can put our energies into full enjoyment of *sensuousness*—life as it is experienced through our five senses and all the joy and beauty they can bring us. We can be kind to ourselves, loving ourselves by such treats as a fragrant bubble bath or oil bath or purchasing a massage shower head, or buying colorful new sheets for our bed—even though we sleep there alone. One single woman says she has always bought herself beautiful nightgowns, lingerie, and lounging robes. "I like them for myself," she says. "Why should a woman feel she deserves to have nice things like that only if a man will see her in them?"

Good question. So many single women have lived limited lives because they felt they deserved nothing more. Psychologist Penelope Russianoff in her book *Why Do I Think I Am Nothing Without a Man?* tells of a friend who had "always felt there was something vacuous and wrong about seeing a sunset—or, for that matter, a dramatic thunderstorm, a sunrise, waves lapping on the beach—without a lover there to validate and enhance the experience" (p. 106). And then, watching the sunset's golds and reds melt together one evening, the woman became so enraptured with the experience *for its own sake* that she completely forgot about the empty feeling of being alone.

I think of the comment my son Dave made years ago as a small child: "I *like* being alone sometimes. It helps you learn to be friends with yourself." Psychiatry professor David Burns, one of the pioneers of cognitive therapy, or mood therapy, for dealing with depression, tells of a "love-addicted" woman who after separation from her husband "failed to treat herself in a caring way," because she had assumed all her life that activities can't be special without someone to share them with. Then one night, she cooked herself a special dinner, decorated the table beautifully, lit candles, and played some of her favorite records on the stereo. She had a delightful evening all alone. "As a result of adopting an active, compassionate attitude toward herself, Janet discovered for the first time in her life that she could not only make it on her own but could really enjoy herself," Dr. Burns writes, adding that Janet's contagious enthusiasm for life resulted in many friends and eventual remarriage *(Feeling Good, p. 280)*.

But one need not limit oneself to special candlelight dinners and outings just for oneself. Why not include a friend? Single persons are often longing for the intimacy, special times, and pleasant memories of activities traditionally associated with, and limited to, romance in the conventional sense. Why not broaden our ideas so that they are not so bound up with obsessive longings for sexual expression, causing us to feel deprived without that expression? We can have good companionship and pleasant times and wonderful emotional intimacy without being bound to the traditional all-or-nothing romantic love script. "It should be clear that both the quantity and quality of your female friendships can vastly enrich your life, serving as a source of companionship and comfort that can act as a buffer against loneliness and can augment, or even substitute for, a relationship with a man," writes Penelope Russianoff in the book quoted earlier (p. 137). Nonsexual friendships with men can enrich our lives too.

But I still want marriage, someone says. Psychology professor I. Ralph Hyatt has some wise advice: "The best way to find a marriage partner is *not* to look for one" *(Before You Love Again, p. 129)*. He suggests that persons concentrate instead on simply enjoying their lives while meeting new people and developing new skills in the process. "Then if you happen to meet someone you'd consider marrying along the way," he writes, "it will be frosting on the cake of a fulfilling life."

We are sexual beings until the day we die. For some persons, genital sexual expression will continue into old age. For others, it will not. But what all of us *can* experience at any stage of life is a sense of being enveloped in God's love and appreciating all God's gifts. And then we can share that love, caring, and joy with others from the deepest levels of our beings. That's what intimacy is all about. And that's what really matters.

BOOKS CITED

Barbach, Lonnie, *For Each Other: Sharing Sexual Intimacy.*
Doubleday & Co., Anchor Books, 1982.

———, *For Yourself: The Fulfillment of Female Sexuality.*
Doubleday & Co., 1975.

——— and Levine, Linda, *Shared Intimacies: Women's Sexual
Experiences.* Doubleday & Co., 1980.

Blackwell, Elizabeth, *The Human Element in Sex: Being a
Medical Inquiry into the Relation of Sexual Physiology to
Christian Morality.* London: J. A. Churchill, 1894. Excerpted
in Nancy Cott (ed.), *The Root of Bitterness.* E. P. Dutton &
Co., 1972.

Burns, David, *Feeling Good: The New Mood Therapy.* William
Morrow & Co., 1980. Quotations are from the Signet paper-
back edition.

Buscaglia, Leo, *Living, Loving, and Learning.* Fawcett, Colum-
bine/Ballantine Books, 1982.

Calderone, Mary, and Johnson, Eric, *The Family Book About
Sexuality.* Harper & Row, Publishers, 1981.

Colton, Helen, *Adults Need Sex Education, Too.* Los Angeles:
Family Forum, 1970.

———, *The Gift of Touch.* Putnam, Seaview Books, 1983.

Federation of Feminist Women's Health Centers, *A New View
of a Woman's Body.* Simon & Schuster, Touchtone Book,
1981.

Fortune, Marie Marshall, *Sexual Violence: The Unmentionable Sin*. Pilgrim Press, 1983.

Glasser, William, *Reality Therapy*. Harper & Row, Perennial Library, 1975.

Gordon, Sol, and Gordon, Judith, *Raising a Child Conservatively in a Sexually Permissive World*. Simon & Schuster, 1983.

Herman, Judith Lewis, *Father-Daughter Incest*. Harvard University Press, 1981.

Hite, Shere, *The Hite Report*. Macmillan Publishing Co., 1976.

Hyatt, I. Ralph, *Before You Love Again*. McGraw-Hill Book Co., 1980.

Kinsey, Alfred C.; Pomeroy, W. B.; Martin, C. E.; and Gebhard, P. H., *Sexual Behavior in the Human Female*. W. B. Saunders Co., 1953.

Lamm, Maurice, *The Jewish Way in Love and Marriage*. Harper & Row, Publishers, 1980.

Maslow, Abraham (ed.), *Motivation and Personality*, 2d ed. Harper & Row, Publishers, 1970.

Masters, William, and Johnson, Virginia, *Human Sexual Inadequacy*. Little, Brown & Co., 1970.

———, *Human Sexual Response*. Little, Brown & Co., 1966.

Money, John, and Ehrhardt, Anke, *Man and Woman, Boy and Girl*. Johns Hopkins University Press, 1972.

Montagu, Ashley, *Touching: The Human Significance of the Skin*, 2d ed. Harper & Row, Colophon Books, 1978.

National Center on Child Abuse and Neglect, *Sexual Abuse of Children*. U.S. Dept. of Health and Human Services, 1980.

Nichols, Mary Gove, "The Murders of Marriage," from T. L. Nichols and Mary Gove Nichols, *Marriage: Its History, Character, and Results; Its Sanctities, and Its Profanities; Its Science and Its Facts*. T. L. Nichols, 1854. Excerpted in Nancy Cott (ed.), *The Root of Bitterness*. E.P. Dutton & Co., 1972.

Pogrebin, Letty Cottin, *Growing Up Free*. McGraw-Hill Book Co., 1980.

Reiss, Ira, *Premarital Sexual Standards in America*. Free Press of Glencoe, 1960.

Russell, Diana E., *Rape in Marriage*. Macmillan Publishing Co., 1982.

Russianoff, Penelope, *Why Do I Think I Am Nothing Without a Man?* Bantam Books, 1983.

Scanzoni, Letha Dawson, *Sex Is a Parent Affair*, rev. ed. Bantam Books, 1982.

—— and Mollenkott, Virginia Ramey, *Is the Homosexual My Neighbor?* Harper & Row, Publishers, 1978.

Shannon, T. W., *Eugenics: The Laws of Sex Life and Heredity*. Mullikin, 1917; replica ed., Doubleday & Co., 1970.

Simon, Sidney, *Caring, Feeling, Touching*. Argus Communications, 1976.

Small, Dwight Hervey, *Christian: Celebrate Your Sexuality*. Fleming H. Revell Co., 1974.

Trible, Phyllis, *God and the Rhetoric of Sexuality*. Fortress Press, 1978.

United Church of Christ, *Human Sexuality: A Preliminary Study*. United Church Press, 1977.

Wolfe, Linda, *The Cosmo Report: Women and Sex in the 80s*. Arbor House Publishing Co., 1981.